AFRICAN WAYS

Recollections of Life in South Africa

by Valerie Poore

ISBN: 9798601730488
Third Edition.

A Rivergirl Publication

For all my faithful blog friends who followed me
in the writing of these memoirs
Anne-Marie Klein, Catherine Marie Glenton, Maria Niku,
Cheryl Stringall, Koos Fernhout, Dale Foster, Margaret
Jevons and many other dear and wonderful friends of the
blogger community

Disclaimer
The contents of this book are the product of my
recollections, and have both inaccuracies as a result of time
passed, and embellishments needed to turn a series of
memories into readable stories. One or two names have
been changed in the interests of discretion, but largely the
people represented are referred to by their given names.
As a result, if there are mistakes regarding the 'characters',
the content or the time, I would like to make it clear that
these are my errors and mine alone. Valerie Poore (Sep
2013)

INTRODUCTION

What made me start writing about African ways? Well, I'd been reading Peter Mayle's Year in Provence. It had given me hours of pleasure in the evenings before bed; on the metro; on the tram; in fact anywhere I could find the excuse to open up where I'd left off and guzzle some more of his appealing, understated wit.

It made me think of my first years in South Africa when I lived on a remote farm in Natal. There's something so refreshingly honest about the countryman's approach to life – and equally often something hilariously funny about it. It doesn't seem to matter whether the setting is in France, Southern Africa or indeed in Cyprus (as in Lawrence Durrell's Bitter Lemons of Cyprus), local characters can make you cry with laughter, weep with sentimental sympathy and even curse the frustrations wrought by their cunning.

Talking to my partner, I started wondering how many stories of my early life in Africa I could collate, and whether they would cross the barriers of time to make the reading as vivid as the memories are still. It was such a culture shock for me as a young woman, fresh from an all mod-cons society in England, to be landed in the wilds of rural South Africa. Everything was so totally different, and at least thirty years behind the life I was used to, if not more.

The result of my musings is the following collection. I can only hope that the love I had and still have for these people, mostly Zulus, is in some way conveyed in the telling. They are stories of the early 1980's when Apartheid was still alive and wielding its ugly brand of discrimination, but on the farm where I lived, the legal fact of the political system was as remote as the mountain slopes against which our farm cottage clung.

What I hope to show through my anecdotes and memories is that first and foremost, the people of South Africa are as colourful, rich and interesting as any other people in the world. They have had a bad press, and the world's media have focused almost solely on the violence and politics of this embattled nation. However, the folk I met in the rural community where I lived were all decent and trustworthy, even if they were sometimes calculating and manipulative, but then aren't we all at times? Above all, though, they were delightful, humorous and generous, and their uncluttered lives gave them an unsophisticated view of the world, which was sometimes devastatingly astute.

These are therefore tales of an outsider's first experience of life in Africa and the fascination of learning - sometimes the hard way- about the all too different approach and attitude to life that the local people had. It begins with my small family's arrival in Pietermaritzburg, the provincial capital of Kwazulu Natal where we found ourselves after a mere month in the country, and ends with our departure from the farm which had been home to us for three glorious years. The stories are not chronological, but follow themes, as memories often do.

By the time we left, life was already changing for me personally and for the whole province. It had been a magical period, if anything because it marked the end of an era of insulation from the political and social upheavals which soon began to permeate even our small community.

It has all gone now. The farms that form the background to these tales have long been vacated. Initially, they were handed over to the Kwazulu government as some form of land deal, but they are now owned by the big forestry companies, and the homes in which we lived are in ruins. I am convinced, however, that the spirit of the people remains the same, and I feel it is even more important that these stories are told if only to demonstrate that South Africa is not just about crime and violence, but also about a wonderful rainbow nation of delightful and hospitable people, who are always ready to laugh in the face of adversity.

CHAPTER 1

First Encounters Of The African Kind

In 1981, it wasn't the Blue train that took passengers in luxury to Natal, South Africa; it was the Red Train. The Blue Train was, and still is, the world famous five star hotel on wheels which travels from Johannesburg to Cape Town.

Nevertheless, the Red Train, which has sadly been discontinued, was a rail journey to experience as well at that time. It was also one of the few means available to car-less travellers for getting to Natal. Being fresh off the plane in South Africa, we had spent most of the last of our precious funds on this wonderful conveyance.

The journey was memorable for its luxury and service, but with only a few hundred Rands left, we were then forced to spend a miserable month in Durban while my partner, Bill, looked for any kind of work available. The ensuing result was that I was now sitting in the Hotel Edward in Pietermaritzburg.

We had left England together with a minimum of baggage and all the enthusiasm of the young and very earnest, and were further accompanied by two very small children. Jodie was just two and Maryssa a mere three months old. The why's and wherefore's are not part of this story, but suffice to say, the coldest winter in years and a struggling business had decided us on this make or break venture to warmer climes.

"I don't mind being poor," I remember telling Bill, "but I do mind being cold as well as poor!" Hence, the idea of Canada in January was discarded, and South Africa was where we found ourselves six weeks after that very heartfelt remark.

I realise now that a touch of irresponsibility is an essential part of being young, as without it no one in their right minds would have left the safety of home and country to venture forth in quest of discovery. Indeed, the world as we know it might have been a much smaller place. Nevertheless, when I think of going to South Africa with no destination, no job, practically no money and two children under three, I often think we must have been touched with a good helping of lunacy.

That being said, there we were in Pietermaritzburg on a January day that made even an oven seem like the cooler option. After weeks of tramping the streets of Durban, Bill had found a job with an automotive paint supplier based in the provincial capital and we had come on a mission to see if we could find somewhere to stay.

Scouring the estate agent's windows had been fruitless, so then we had despairingly looked through the local papers. Finally, tucked in amongst ads for cattle feed, skin lightener and ghastly plastic furniture, we had seen a very small ad indeed. It read, "Flat to rent on farm. Furnished. Reasonable rent."

Bill had phoned the number given, and had spoken to a charming but elderly Dutch woman, who had kindly offered to come and see us that evening at the hotel. So, there I was, waiting.

'Ouma' Ellens, as she quickly became known (Ouma being the Afrikaans for Grandma), was the mother every one has always wanted. She was as round as she was tall, with a kindly face wreathed in good humour and practical compassion. She also suffered from severe hip problems and despite having had one operation for a replacement prosthesis, she told us she was due for another and leaned heavily on a stick.

Still, nothing daunted, she'd found her way up to our hotel room and promptly made herself at home by sitting on the bed with Jodie cuddled up to her instant granny.

"You can't keep these children here," she scoffed at me as soon as she'd swallowed some tea.

"I'm…um…," was about all I managed in response before she launched into a full description of the flat they'd advertised and how suitable it would be for the children.

Apparently, the flat was in fact a cottage that they'd had built for their son when he got married, but the son and his wife moved out – as children do – and it had been standing empty for several months.

At the end of her glowing description, she finally mentioned how happy she would be if we'd take it because she and her husband were leaving for the US the following day on a six-month tour – the hip replacement being put on hold as an inconvenience - and they would be much relieved if the flat, which was attached to the old farmhouse, was occupied.

I gulped. Bill was still out and we had no clue where the farm was, but at the rent – an incredible R70 per month – it seemed like a dream come true.

"OK," I managed to gasp, and with that, she beamed effusively, heaved herself to her feet, and started for the door.

9

"Oh yes, I forgot to say, you can use the dinger while we're away. That way you won't get stuck there while your man's at work. Call my neighbour Gwen for the key when you move in." And without explaining further, off she went.

Somewhat shell shocked, I finally realised I'd agreed to rent the flat, but still didn't know where it was and had no clue where to find the said Gwen. Nor did I know what the dinger was or what it would prevent me from being stuck to. My brain went tilt a tad.

When Bill got back, we risked a further phone call. All was revealed. What we hadn't appreciated before was that in the wilds of the Natal countryside, the phone lines were all still party lines. Every call went through the local exchange, and each household on the line had a different series of beeps, a bit like morse code, as a call signal. The neighbour Gwen answered the call this time as, it transpired, she always did when the Ellenses were out, because of course, everyone knew everyone else's code.

She knew all about us already – no surprise with such an effective grape vine - and even seemed to know we were moving in before we did. We could come out and see the flat the following evening, and she would give us all the keys, including the one for the dinger which turned out to be the Ellenses' pick-up truck, or *bakkie*. Why it was called a dinger we had still to find out.

"Isn't she being very trusting?" asked Bill. "I mean, they don't know us...we could be con men or anything."

"She'll have made up her mind about you in thirty seconds," Gwen assured him. "That's why she wanted to come and see you in 'Maritzburg," she explained, using the abbreviated from for the provincial capital. "If Pauline Ellens says you're alright, you are." And with that vote of confidence, we arranged to call in at her cottage near the farmhouse the following evening after Bill had finished work.

We were elated. What a stroke of incredible luck. At the rent they were asking we could afford to live decently, and just think of all that wonderful fresh air and food for the children. Ouma Ellens had told me that they kept cows for their milk, cream and butter and that Oupa (grandpa) was a keen vegetable gardener, so we could help ourselves to anything we liked. And now we were going to have it all to ourselves too.

We decided to go down to the restaurant and celebrate.

When people talk about African time, there really is truth in what they say. If you think about it, the Spaniards have their siesta, and the French their two to three-hour lunch breaks, but in Africa where it's really hot, there is no such acknowledgement of the sapping power of the midday sun.

To compensate, however, there is a different time scale to life, which means that everything is done at half pace to conserve the energy necessary for drinking, partying and having fun later on at the local *shebeen*, an informal and definitely unlicensed type of pub. Very sensible under the circumstances.

We didn't really understand African time when we arrived in South Africa, but by the time we'd got to 'Maritzburg, we had at least learnt that we needn't expect our requests for service to receive the prompt and rather frenetic response we had become used to in England. That was fine. It was very hot, and we could quite understand why people should want to take life at a marginally more leisurely pace than we were accustomed to.

We were thus quite unprepared for the ministrations of the awesome Innocent the Great.

Innocent was our waiter in the restaurant that night, but he should have been on stage. He was brilliant, and quite without equal. Despite being lively, though, he managed to maintain an unflappable cool quite worthy of the most practiced 'African timer'.

We only discovered later on that many South African mothers give their children European names, but instead of choosing traditional or even Christian names, they simply find words they like and use those. As many South Africans are also devoted Christians, words such as 'virtue', and 'honesty' are very popular. 'Innocent' didn't really suit our man given the suggestions of a life spent on the entertainment circuit, but it wasn't a name one would forget.

His skill was in the way he managed all the tables simultaneously, not only delivering plates of food but laying new covers, clearing dirty dishes and providing drinks with what appeared to be a seamless vaudeville act.

The restaurant at the hotel was a rather stately high walled room, cooled by great swishing ceiling fans and soft air from the tall casement windows. Its air of subdued grace was further enhanced by the beige figured silk that covered the walls and the starched white cloths on the dark gleaming tables.

There were only a few of us eating that night, but conversation was totally suspended as all of us, the children included, watched the performance of Innocent the Great with baited breath. In fact we were waiting for something to go wrong and dreaded the possible damage to our elegant surroundings, but quite astonishingly, it didn't.

What he did was worthy of an award, given his size and shape. Innocent was extremely tall with skin the colour of polished chestnuts and a lanky frame supported by enormous feet.

Unexpectedly adroit, he weaved between the chairs and deftly frisbeed both clean and full plates on to precise spots on the tables, while removing dirty ones before they landed. How he managed to co-ordinate these activities without so much as a chink of contact, let alone any breakages must have been the result of years of dedicated training.

I tried to imagine the crockery cost of his early practice sessions.

Nevertheless, when we applauded one particularly brilliant manoeuvre, we were treated to a withering glare which we had to presume was because we'd transgressed his ideas of what was dignified. Because dignified he was. Very.

Innocent was also the master of the dining room. He decided what we were going to eat, which happened to be quite contrary to our own ideas.

The ordering went something like this:

Innocent: And what does *Madaam* like to eat?

Me: Well, I'd like the fish please, Innocent.

Innocent: Oh no, *Madaam*, the fish not good today, I will order the Chicken for *Madaam*, and now you *Sair*?

Bill: I'd like a T-bone steak, medium rare, please

Innocent: Ah, bad choice, *Sair*, the chef, he not cook T-bone enough, you have the fillet. Much better. For the *childrenn*, I get the fish sticks and chips. And you will have a bowl of salad for your health. Thank you *Sair*, *Madaam*.

And without giving us time to protest, off he went to arrange our meals. It was our first experience of eating out in South Africa, but it was a good indication of what was to come in a country where people eat with the same enthusiasm as they do everything else.

The chicken, when it arrived, was a complete small bird, roasted to perfection, and served with small crunchy roast potatoes and sweet caramelised carrots. Bill's steak covered his entire plate and was tender to the cut, while the children's fish sticks were full, fluffy and flaky. The salad was crisp, slick with dressing and full of feta cheese, crunchy peppers and croutons. Both the wine and beer were South African and excellent.

Innocent presided over our meal with the care of one who had a stake in our well-being, which of course he did, but his attention was such that we had no reservations about tipping him more than the customary ten percent. The resulting grin we received was like a shaft of sunlight and we realised we'd been privileged to witness a rare event: the smile of Innocent the Great.

The following evening we set off for the farm around six. It was still light when we left, but as with all latitudes of around thirty degrees and below on either side of the equator, darkness descends with almost unnerving speed.

Driving in South Africa had its own surprises. Luckily for those of us from the UK, they drive on the left as we do, but there are other challenges to take into account.

On one of our first trips out with a colleague of Bill's, we were speeding along the highway into Durban when to my astonishment, I saw what I was convinced was a person scuttling across the three lanes to the central reservation.

As we flashed past, I was even more dumbstruck to see that I was indeed right. Sure enough, there was a middle aged, print-frocked and head-scarfed woman poised with one hand on the barrier, ready to make a dash across the other three lanes of this fast moving motorway.

Bill's colleague, Mike, seemed to be either oblivious or totally unimpressed by this piece of derring-do, so I asked him in some concern whether he had seen the woman.

"Sure," came the reply, "you see it all the time along here."

He went on to explain that the section of highway along which we were travelling passed through one of the most heavily populated areas of Natal. The area to the north was called the Valley of the Thousand Hills and was densely covered with African kraals and villages. When the highway was built, it effectively cut off the villages to the south from their neighbours on the other side.

"What would you do," he asked, "if you lived on one side of the highway, and all your relatives lived on the other side?" Before the road was built, they had just walked across a few fields and they were with their folks. The construction of a six-lane highway with bridges only every ten k's or so, had turned what was once a one or two kilometre walk into a fifteen to twenty-kilometre trek. "Remember, hardly any of the villagers have cars," Mike pointed out. "In their shoes, I think I might chance it too!"

I felt suitably humbled by this matter-of-fact explanation, and as the months passed, we quickly became used to seeing all manner of oddities on the highways, including bicycles and even the occasional donkey and cart.

That evening as we were heading out of Pietermaritzburg, the sun was in our eyes, and we were more focused on looking out for the road signs we needed to follow than on the interesting array of fellow travellers.

Our directions took us to the Edendale road, which we were instructed to follow in the direction of Impendle. Somewhere around the village of Boston, we would see a turning towards Elandskop, where we would again turn off in the direction of Byrne.

Edendale was the African township which sprawled the hillsides out of 'Maritzburg. In those days, it was an irregular collection of tin shacks, *rondavels*, small brick houses and ramshackle smallholdings. Donkeys, goats, sheep and chickens competed for the thin grass, which only barely held the rust coloured soil from eroding away completely. Nevertheless, the land was scarred with deep *dongas* (open cracks), which told their own story of the erosion caused by overgrazing and over crowding.

People were walking or pushing barrows and bikes but mostly they gathered in clusters, talking at the tops of their voices, even though they were only two face widths apart from each other. One thing a born and bred Natalian knows how to do is project.

We were to learn that this skill comes from years of standing on hilltops conversing with a cousin, brother or buddy on a similar hilltop on the other side of the valley, which could of course be several kilometres away.

By the time we were through Edendale, it was lighting up time, and complete darkness followed soon after. It was then that I began to get nervous.

What started it was the road signs. At intervals we would see curious instructions such as: Slow *Stadig* and then an image of something that looked like the outline of a huge shouldered monster with the words Only *Slegs* underneath.

16

What did this mean? What was a *stadig* and a *sleg*? We were in Africa, so it could be anything. I had, however, forgotten that being in a country with two official languages meant that all public notices and signs would be in both Afrikaans and English.

We hadn't seen these particular signs before because we'd only been on the highway, so we didn't make the connection that in fact *stadig* simply meant 'slow' and that *slegs* was the Afrikaans for 'only', meaning that the sign only referred to the vehicles shown in the image – in this case, my monster was a tractor, which of course later became quite clear.

At that moment, though, these warning signs seemed loaded with menace.

Then, even worse, the road to Elandskop and beyond was not tarred. I had never been on a dirt road in my life, so as we bumped, lurched and wound our way up into the foothills of the Drakensburg mountains, I became increasingly convinced that we were heading into some kind of jungle.

It was quite obvious to me that we were going to die out there. I could just imagine the headlines: "English breakfast for Lion family" for in my hopelessly fertile imagination, there were certainly lions and tigers ready to leap out at us from every tree.

Bill, ever practical, pointed out gently that for one thing, there were no tigers in Africa, and for another we'd hardly be likely to find a respectable, old Dutch couple living in the middle of a wild animal reserve with no better protection than the ubiquitous and rusty two-stringed barbed-wire fence. He had a point.

But I was not to be comforted. To add to my trepidation there was a violent electrical storm which had suddenly descended upon us as we'd left the relative civilisation (three houses and a post office) of Elandskop. For anyone with even the slightest fear of thunderstorms, the first experience of what is a daily occurrence in Africa in summer will remain indelibly imprinted on the psyche. In England, I had crawled under beds at the first rumble of thunder.

By the time we saw the sign for 'Cottingham Farm' swinging from an old five-barred gate, I was a sweating, nauseous wreck.

We pulled gratefully in through the gateway, and by the time we'd drawn up in front of the house and switched off the engine, there was a woman standing by the car door holding a powerful flashlight.

It was Gwen of the phone call. A straight, slim and handsome woman, she had that no-nonsense air about her that made me want to give up all pretence of being an adult and fall gibbering and blubbering into her arms. Fortunately, I still had some restraint.

She and her husband lived in a cottage a couple of hundred metres back along the road. In my own fantasy bubble of fear, I hadn't noticed it, but she had seen us passing and had decided to meet us at the house. Privately, I thought we must have been obvious as the newcomers as we crept tentatively along the road. The only other cars we'd seen had been a couple of *bakkies* hurtling along at breakneck speed, which I imagined was the customary pace for the locals.

We had parked in front of the old farmhouse, and even in the velvety blackness of the rural night, I could see that it was one of those wonderful spreading single story homes, surrounded on all sides by graceful verandas. We walked round to one side, where there appeared to be a newer structure attached to the end of the old house, and it was into this addition that we went.

Entering through a stable style door, we found ourselves in an attractive modern kitchen fitted out with pine cupboards and counters. It was lit softly by oil lamps, and it was only then that I found out there was no electricity. Now bearing in mind that I had only been out of England once before, and that was just a two-week tour of France and Spain staying in hostelries which were modest, but with full mod cons, I wasn't really equipped for life without things I could switch on and off at will.

On the other hand, the soft pools of light around the oil lamps were very attractive, and the kitchen anyway seemed to be fitted with everything needed for home comforts. There was a stove that used bottled gas, a large fridge that Gwen said was fuelled by paraffin, a modern steel sink and draining board, ample cupboards and a long breakfast bar with stools dividing the kitchen from the living area. There was also a huge walk-in pantry with its own window to keep the food stocks well aired. All this was encouraging, so despite my initial misgivings, I was happy to be led through the kitchen to the large living room beyond.

When Gwen carried a lamp through to cast more light on the living area, I was further cheered to see that the room had been designed like a swiss chalet. The Ellenses had dispensed with a ceiling in favour of pine boards which followed the pitch of the roof, giving a lovely lofty volume to the room.

Directly beyond the kitchen was the dining area with a chrome framed table and chairs, but then an interior wall ended to allow the lounge the full width of the cottage with wide picture windows on both sides. With its parquet flooring and large open fireplace, it seemed luxurious beyond anything I had imagined. There was already a rather stylish, oak framed sofa and matching chairs, together with a small round coffee table on a square Persian rug. I loved it, and kept repeating "All this for seventy Rands a month!" like a kind of mantra inside my head.

The geyser in the pristine white bathroom was also fed by bottled gas, so apart from lights and the lack of a TV (which I certainly didn't mind), we would have everything we needed. There was even a plentiful supply of cutlery, crockery and pots in the kitchen. By the time we took a look at the two bedrooms that led off the passage from the kitchen, I was sold. I didn't care if there were lions and tigers sniffing round the back door. I wanted it.

Bill and I looked at each other and nodded. When could we move in? Immediately, said Gwen. We arranged with her that we should start bringing our meagre possessions out the next day, and be installed by the weekend. How could our fortunes possibly improve?

CHAPTER 2

The Farm

A Real Dust Up

Our first real sight of the farm that was to be our home for the next three years came the day after we had thrown caution to the figurative wildlife and committed ourselves to living there.

We thought it might be wise to see exactly what our surroundings looked like in daylight, so Bill took a couple of hours off and borrowed a car to drive us back out to Cottingham. We approached it from the Richmond direction this time as a test to see which was the best route. Watching the sweeping green fields of rich agricultural land, we decided that even if this was a bit further round than the Edendale road, it was infinitely more comforting in its demonstrably cultivated domesticity. These were properly organised and nurtured acres and much more 'European' in their style.

Turning on to the dirt road that marked the approach to the village of Byrne, we rolled along happily with our car windows down. The road climbed and then dipped towards the village that was famous for its settler origins and as we passed Byrne's small settlement on the right hand side, we were charmed to see neat cottages surrounded by incongruously English country gardens. There was also a lych-gate entrance to the village church on the left, and the whole impression was one of cosy stability.

My images of snack hunting wildlife began to fade, and I was able to appreciate the magnificence of the mountain foothills we were beginning to scale. After leaving Byrne, we started a slow but steady ascent, only occasionally relieved by slight dips as the road curved round a rocky outcrop or even an old tree. Euphoria, no … Utopia set in – only to be smashed a moment later when we were enveloped in a cloud of dust which we seemed to be eating in chunks.

The reason for this sudden engulfment was a battered looking *bakkie* careering down the mountain without any apparent concern for anyone coming in the opposite direction. We were soon to learn that this was to be expected and trained ourselves to react accordingly by hurtling equally fast in the opposite direction ourselves so as to avoid the mushroom clouds of dust. We also learnt to anticipate and respond smartly to the peremptory command "Windows!!" by furiously winding up everything that could be closed at record speeds.

Once the air had cleared, and we had emerged coughing and spluttering into the sunshine again, we were entranced by the views glimpsed through the gaps in the hills, and as we climbed on up, the panorama spread out below us in an awe inspiring spread of rank upon rank of hills culminating in the dominant crags of the Drakensberg mountain range in the distance.

By the time we reached the farm we were more than ever convinced that we'd arrived in heaven and that all this was meant to be.

The Tennis Club

Moving in didn't take long. We didn't have much of anything, and in any event everything we needed was there. More importantly, though, we had to familiarise ourselves with the area and in particular, the people who lived around us.

The Ellenses had gone and we had to sort ourselves out, or rather, I had to do the sorting because in fact, Bill was away all day and I was alone on the farm with two small children. Gwen and her husband, Eric, were my life savers. They took me to meet some of the local farmers and their families, the nearest of whom lived about four miles away and happened to be their daughter, Moreen and her husband.

In fact, many of the local families were related, either by marriage or by ancestry. The whole district was originally populated by the settler families who were also those responsible for establishing the village of Byrne. As I understood it, many of these settlers had been connected to the Beaulieu estate in southern England, and the family lines had continued.

One of the first things we had to do as part of our social integration was to join the Tennis Club, which met every weekend at a small clubhouse in the valley and which sported two clay courts. The Tennis club also housed the local library, so it was a further incentive to go, because no tennis, no reading. And reading had become somewhat essential in a world without television or stereos. Given that I have never been able to find a tennis racquet that didn't immediately sprout holes for the balls to whistle through, there had to be something more in it for me and I

23

was only too happy to immerse myself in the books while the others played, or tried to play, formal matches.

The way it was organised was also very formal. Each week, one of the husbands would organise the matches and the wife would make the tea – all terribly proper and terribly English. They didn't call Natal the Last Outpost for nothing, and that term of endearment was no doubt based on the stoic loyalty to solid British traditions of such small communities as these. Everyone wore proper 'whites'; everyone behaved with formal courtesy; everyone stopped for a tea of sandwiches, cake and cream scones at 3p.m (none of this twenty-four-hour clock nonsense); then everyone resumed play until the best couple won; finally, everyone slapped each other heartily on the back, shook hands, complimented each other on a good day's play, collected their week's reading and went home. As I said, all terribly proper. That is, until Bill came along.

On the occasion in question, it was our week to organise the matches and make the tea. I had been dreading it, as I had never been much of a cake maker, so confined myself to making scones and buns along with the thinly sliced sandwiches. Rather proud of my efforts, I was busily laying out the tea on the trestle tables which had been placed on the club veranda, when I heard Bill giving his idea of instructions for the afternoon.

As always, he was suitably vague in his directives and seemed to be failing to give the players a proper order of play. To this day, I don't know if he really misunderstood the question or not, but knowing his tendency to irreverence for traditions, I have my suspicions. The conversation began with one of the players asking, "So, William, what's the order of play?"

His tone was just sufficiently pompous to rile Bill, who couldn't stand being called William, and I could hear the irritation in his voice when he answered, "Well, Peter, you're playing with Julia (or Sonia or whatever) and Sonia (or whoever) is playing with Frank (and so on)."

Peter was not one for sensitivity, and his antenna were clearly not in operation when he pursued the point. "No, no, William, what we mean is HOW are we playing?

Well, that was too much for Bill to resist. "How do you play?" he asked, voice loaded with innocence. "How? Well, you take your bat, and you throw up your ball…"

By now, I'd emerged from the tea-room and had spotted not only the mischievous glint in his eye, but the appalled look in the eyes of the players. A bat? He'd called a tennis racquet a bat? This was outrageous. Not only had he insulted their intelligence but even worse than that, he had no clue about order of play.

Well, that was it, we were never asked to organise games again, and were never really accepted into the club circle after that, but we didn't care. As long as we could get our books each week, we had no problem with being the misfits of the Elandskop tennis club. I could have kissed him on the spot for so unpardonable a *faux pas*.

Milking the situation

Adjacent to the farmhouse and cottage where we lived were a few small, enclosed paddocks which were retained by the Ellenses for their own use, while the remainder of their fifteen-hundred-acre farm had been sold to one of the neighbouring ranchers. These paddocks housed two cows whose milk provided the house and us with our daily needs, but of course, now the occupants of the house were away, it fell to me to make sure everything continued running smoothly.

Now, one of a cow's daily necessities is to rid itself of excess milk. Failure to do this is extremely uncomfortable for the said cow, which will let you know in no uncertain terms that it is in fact busting an udder.

Within a couple of days of moving in, we had learnt enough about the routines of the household to know that the cows were milked every morning at around nine by the Ellenses' general factotum, Kheswa. He resembled nothing more closely than a walnut wearing a hat, whose shell was occasionally split into a devastatingly white grin. Other than that, he was small, wiry and probably very strong, but he liked to make an issue of being thin so that he could avoid doing anything too taxing. The running of the Ellenses' reduced holdings was definitely a family affair as Kheswa's daughter, Bongile, ran the house itself and his son, David, was the herd boy. No doubt the other ten children were employed in some capacity or other too, but I didn't see them other than in the distance riding the farm ponies.

Each day, Kheswa would stagger, wheezing and puffing, up the farm path from the shed about fifty metres from the house, carrying a large galvanised bucket full to the brim with frothy creamy milk.

I would then take about two litres straight from the bucket for our normal requirements, and Bongile, who was the complete opposite of her sinewy father, helped herself to her own generous share. The remainder of the bucket was left for the cream to rise to the top and then we would skim it off and use it for thick cream or to make butter, and buttermilk. It seems incredible now, but we did actually use it all – every day.

26

What happened to the rest of what the cows produced I never asked, but looking back, I expect it was part of the daily rations given out to old man Kheswa and his extended family. The cows were not milked in the evenings as the calves were put back with them until the end of the day, and then removed from their mums over night.

After a week or so of observing all this from a distance, I wandered down to the shed one morning to watch Kheswa do the milking. It was all done by hand, and so I looked on with interest as he chattered away to me, grinning his rather charming gapped tooth smile and occasionally licking away the spit that formed because he had so few teeth to keep it in. His hat bobbed up and down as he talked, innocently oblivious to the fact I had no idea what he was saying.

Then suddenly, he leapt up and motioned firmly for to me to sit down on the upturned crate he was using for the task of milking. It was only then that I realised all his chatter had been an explanation of how to milk the beast in question, and that now it was my turn to try. Talk about instant trepidation.

I made feeble gestures to show I wasn't quite ready for so weighty a responsibility, but he was so insistent that I lowered myself reluctantly onto the crate and looked at him imploringly. Spitting out a gob of the tobacco he was chewing, Kheswa knelt down beside me, and with deft movements showed me what to do. Squeeze, pull down, squeeze, pull down, squeeze etc all the time making sort of turning movements with his hands so that the milk was drawn to the end of the teat.

I was reminded of one of those frustration dreams where one tries to hold on to a soap covered balloon full of water, while trying to squeeze it at the same time, and then constantly having it slip from one's grasp. I'm sure the sensation of milking a cow is exactly the same. My hands just kept sliding off the end of the teat, and try as I might, I could get no more out of that udder than a few paltry drips. Even the cow turned round and looked at me in disgust. It took Kheswa about fifteen minutes to milk one animal completely. It would take me ten times as long if I had to go on at this rate.

Smiling at him in embarrassed guilt, I got up, shrugged my shoulders and thanked the Lord that I didn't have to do this for a living. The dairy industry would grind to a standstill. I should have known better. Kheswa was a wily old soul and had more than a few tricks up his ragged sleeve.

The next morning, I started hearing the mournful bellowing of a cow in distress round about nine thirty. It kept up its plaintiff howl for about ten minutes before I thought I'd better go and have a look. Hooking one infant into one arm and grabbing the other by a small hand, we set off down the path to the milking shed.

There, to my concern, were the two cows standing at the closed shed door, as if waiting to go inside – which is in fact what they were doing. They hadn't been fetched for milking and being creatures of habit as they were, they had gone to the shed themselves to find some relief from their bursting glands. Unfortunately, there was no one there, and it was about this that they were complaining bitterly as we approached.

I didn't really know how serious it would be if a cow were not milked on time. I suppose the logical answer would have been to let the calves loose with them, but not knowing any of this then, I was worried by the interruption in their routine.

Back at the house, I called Bongile outside and explained the situation as simply as possible. Bongile knew some English, but it had its limits, so I was surprised when she said, "Don't worry Mama, I call him for you," and with that she set off into the garden. However, far from heading off home to her kraal, which was what I thought she was going to do, she stopped, cupped her hands round her mouth and with a bellow that began in her stomach, she hurled a thunderous "*yebo*" across the valley towards the hills beyond.

It was a wonderful cry, full of the throaty yearning of Africa - that is as long as you were standing at least five metres away. I was standing right next to her and so practically keeled over from this vocal assault, only to hear just seconds later an answering "*yebo*" ringing its way back to us.

Bongile cupped her hands to her mouth again, but this time I was prepared. Scooping up the children, I beat a hasty retreat into the cottage and left this African version of a modern WiFi network to finish exchanging information. Who needs technology when you have such an effective communication system? You never get downtime problems with this method either.

A few minutes later, she came smiling to the door. "Ah, Mama, my sister she say that Kheswa is sick. He take too many pillies."

"My goodness, Bongi, is he alright? Why did he do that? Shouldn't he be in hospital?" I had visions of the poor old soul overdosed and comatose.

"No, no, Mama, Kheswa, he must stay on toilet, he take too many pillies for his belly." And with that she started to roll with laughter. "And so, Mama must milk the cows today. Kheswa, he say she know how." Peals of laughter again. She took herself off throwing another amused chuckle over her shoulder, and then I realised what was going on.

For whatever reason he thought fit, Kheswa had taken too many of the favourite local *muti* (medicine), which was a powerful laxative commonly known as 'pillies'. They often need this assistance with their internal plumbing, due to the amount of *mealie pap* (maize porridge) they consume. The results meant that of course Kheswa could not make the walk over to the farm, and that having 'taught' me how to milk the cows, I should now be able to relieve him whenever he was out of sorts or, more probably, wanted some time off. As I said, he was a wily old soul.

I can only give thanks that there was no one to see me mauling those poor beasts that morning as I painfully extracted enough liquid from them to ensure they were relieved of pressure and that we had enough milk for the day. It took me two whole hours, while the cows demonstrated commendable patience at being yanked around by such a crass amateur. Every now and then the victim in question would look back at me with a long-suffering sigh and moo plaintively.

When I'd done as much as I felt necessary, I turned the cows loose with their calves, who must have thought they'd been sent to their favourite café where milk was being served in bottomless cups for the day. For myself, I was dirty, sweaty and exhausted, but rather pleased that I had in fact managed to do it without injuring either myself or the cows.

I never did master the art of milking, though, and to this day would love to know how some people manage to do it so quickly and make it look so easy. Is it simply a question of practice, or is there some special training involving water filled balloons covered in soap?

Matters of Security

On the remote farms in Natal, there was a special kind of early warning system to alert the farmers to the approach of possible cattle thieves or house breakers. This worked in just a semi-wireless fashion in that it combined both bush and techno telegraph.

Nearly all the homes along the mountain and valley were fitted with CB radios. These were vital when communicating emergencies such as *veld* fires or cattle break outs, but they were also used in a kind of neighbourhood watch fashion. However, this on its own would not have worked, and needed that extra element of African sensory perception to go along with it.

I discovered how it really operated one evening while the Ellenses were still away. As was normal, Bill and I had gone through the usual routines of lighting the oil lamps and bathing and bedding children. We were sitting listening to a radio play on our favourite national station, Springbok Radio, when following a knock on the door I opened it to a serious looking Kheswa bearing an unaccustomed air of command and a wheezing chest. After inviting him into the kitchen where he stood getting his breath back and fingering his hat, his walnut head looking strangely naked, he told us that he'd had a message from his cousin on the neighbouring farm. There were suspicious movements, his cousin had said. A *bakkie* was driving too slowly and carefully along our road without its lights on.

Why, I asked, was this so suspicious? Maybe the *bakkie's* lights just didn't work. "No, Mama," said Kheswa, his mouth working with the effort of speaking English, "my cousin, he say that the lights, they go off now, then on, but, Mama, they more off than on." He illustrated his words by opening and closing his fist several times, just to make sure I understood that this was a headlight he was talking about. "You call Mr Bruce. Very important, Mama. He know what to do. You call him on the seebee."

I was still not convinced. How did his cousin know all this from a far-off farm, and why did I have to use the 'seebee.' With growing agitation at my stupidity, Kheswa explained briefly that his cousin lived on the homestead at the foot of the valley, which was in fact the house belonging to the new owner of the farm, Tony. They were away for the evening leaving Kheswa's cousin on guard, and he had seen this happening from his vantage point at the base of the slopes.

Acting on impulse, he'd mounted a pony and dashed up the hill to Kheswa's kraal to deliver the message and dashed back again so as not to desert his post for too long. Kheswa had then come hot-footing over to us to take action. Since he had never used a phone in his life, but knew all about the CB radios the farmers had in their own *bakkies* it seemed the logical thing to do, especially if 'Mr Bruce' himself was out.

Bill then took Kheswa to the porch by the backdoor of the main house where the CB was installed for a quick lesson in its use, and made contact with our neighbour, who was suitably impressed that these 'poms' (as we English were known) had been so pro-active.

He then did whatever was required to prevent any nefarious activities taking place, which probably entailed tearing after the culprits in his truck, hurling loud and threatening abuse at them if, indeed, they hadn't already taken flight, and ensuring they left the way they'd come. In our turn we were suitably impressed by Kheswa's initiative, which had almost definitely averted either a burglary or a cattle theft.

This was not the end of Kheswa's security conscious activities though. Some months later, we were lying asleep in bed one night, when we were awoken to the roar of a diesel engine. Bill flew out of bed uttering wild expletives about who, where and how he was going to deal with the perpetrator of this crime, and scrambling into the bare necessities he grabbed a flashlight and charged out into the night.

The ensuing events went something like this: When he emerged from the cottage, Bill looked down towards the sheds and saw the farm tractor being revved up noisily with its lights full on. It then started to lurch forwards in a drunken fashion and Bill was convinced someone was about to take off with it.

Not stopping to think that this was rather unusual behaviour for a criminal, he armed himself with a kitchen broom and keeping the flashlight off, tore down across the paddock to reach the gate to the road before the tractor got there. Then, as it approached him, he stood in front of it, switched the flashlight on and pointed it straight into the eyes of the tractor thief, while beating a harsh tattoo on the engine cover with the broom stick.

From inside the cab, came a piercing howl of terrified anguish and next, there was a body tumbling out of the door, which promptly tried to get up and run away.

Fortunately, the tractor had stalled, otherwise Bill would have been mincemeat, but instead he was able to leap after the body and grab it by the scruff of the neck, push it to the ground and sit on it.

Imagine Bill's horror when he found the body was in fact Kheswa, or at least a trembling, terrified form of Kheswa, and one who smelled strongly of alcohol.

When he was finally coherent, it transpired that Kheswa had thought Bill was some kind of *sangoma* (spiritual healer) with a grudge, a misconception explained by the eerie appearance the torch light had given his uplit features. As soon as had persuaded the old man he wasn't the witch doctor come to cast a spell on him, Bill asked him what on earth he was doing with the tractor.

"Ah, Mr Bill, I drink a little much this night so I sleep in the shed here. I not go home. And then I wake up. I need to go outside and then my eyes they see a bad man in the place of the master's vegetables. Kheswa think the man he is taking the vegetable of the master, so I want to make him run. But here I have no horse, but the *gunda gunda* (tractor), he a good horse too, so I think I make bad man run with the *gunda gunda*. But then you come, Mr Bill, and now he gone anyway."

Bill praised Kheswa for his bravery, silently thanking whichever gods were in charge that night that he hadn't got any further than the farm gate. Then he helped him back to the hut and covered him with a blanket again before leaving him for the night.

On the way back to the cottage, Bill passed the 'place of the master's vegetables'. The only thing there was a scarecrow I had erected the day before to keep the birds off the fully-grown lettuces and beans. It looked distinctly like a very bad and evil man and, maybe even worse, after a few drinks it quite probably took on a life of its own.

CHAPTER 3

Drought

In European countries, we have the luxury of knowing only brief and sporadic periods of water shortage, but in Africa it is a fact of life and the times of plentiful water are usually short lived.

Coming from England's West Country, which is notoriously wet and lush, I was totally unaccustomed to having to ration my water consumption to the point where our worth was measured by the number of uses we could find for a single basin full of the stuff. It took some getting used to, but the first few months of autumn and winter taught us all we needed to know, because it turned into one of the longest spells of drought the region had suffered for years.

The first warning signs came when we heard from neighbours that their bore holes were running dry and they would have to consider investing in further drilling. In our case, we had a large tank on a solid concrete pedestal outside our kitchen door, which was fed from a usually strong spring up in the mountain behind us. It relied totally on gravity and a floater system to regulate its level, and until midway through the autumn month of May, I had been happily unaware of the need to conserve water, as there had always been a plentiful flow. In fact no one had yet thought to mention that this could be otherwise.

In the latter months of the summer, there had been very little rain, and our now indispensable neighbour, Gwen, had been complaining that her garden was suffering from thirst. Having adopted her as mentor, guide, granny and confidante all rolled into one, I had spent many afternoons sitting on the sun-filled balcony of her Swiss style chalet discussing the needs of the different indigenous plants and birds, but the subject of our own water supply just didn't arise. And so, I carried on squandering our precious resource, cheerfully oblivious of what was to come.

In most parts of South Africa, the rain falls in the spring and summer months, the autumn and winter being largely bone dry, so I should have realised that if there had been less than average rain that year, it spelt potential problems.

My first inkling that trouble was on the way was when I noticed that the evening water pressure was somewhat feeble, just when I needed to bath two normally very grubby children. However, I was deceived and relieved to find by the morning that the pressure was back up to normal again and so dismissed it until the evening when the same nagging concern would be prompted over again.

I happened to mention this one day to Tony, the energetic and amiable owner of the farm, who always seemed to be dashing about and rarely stopped to indulge in social chitchat. As a result, my remarks were intended more as something to say than from any deep-seated anxiety. However, I was shaken from my complacence when he regarded me thoughtfully, uttering the typical Natalian expression of doubt, "Ya, well, no, fine, we'd better take a look at that. If you're running low then so will my cattle and that'll be real problem. Might have to make a plan." I was to hear him use this last phrase so many times in the future that it was hardly a surprise when I later found it had actually spread out of Natal and gone national. In fact 'make a plan' is simply the standard filler phrase for any situation that needs action.

Meantime, I was chastened to hear that Tony's cattle appeared to mean more to him than a young family with small children, but I had not yet learned that the farmers' preoccupation with water far exceeds any other concern. It even assumes more importance in their lives than their favourite four-wheel drive *bakkies*, which is saying something considering they seemed to be permanently glued to the steering wheels of these hardy beasts.

In England it wasn't done to go traipsing across a farmer's land, so I'd never crossed the fields to look for the source of our household water. When I asked Tony where we'd find it, he threw out a brawny arm in the direction of the mountain behind us. "It's over the...re," he said, the word 'there' being extended to fit the distance involved.

It seemed that in place of offering actual estimations, the length of the word 'there' provided quite an accurate indication of measurement. For example, if pronounced normally it would suggest something within arm's reach. A slight emphasis on the long syllable would extend that to the end of the room, and so on. By the time you were talking about a farm on the other side of the valley, the word had stretched to quite mammoth proportions. In this case, I guessed we were talking about a mere couple of hundred metres.

I followed Tony through the paddocks that rose behind the farmhouse until we reached the first of the dams that were dug into the side of the hill. The stream that fed it was also the one that fed our tank, and on closer inspection we saw it had dwindled from its normal merry rush to a sluggish, greasy dribble. On the outlet side of the dam, it was even more depressing. There appeared to be just a seepage coming down the hill towards the house. I reflected in some dismay that it was no wonder there was so little pressure after we'd been using the water all day. The fact that the situation had improved by the morning was explained by the fact that when sleeping, we weren't eating. Or washing. Or cleaning. Or flushing toilets.

As I thought about all these activities for which we used the water, I gained my first insight into what a precious commodity it is, and how I had taken it so much for granted. Up till that moment.

Tony contemplated the apathetic traces of what used to be our lively stream. Then, he gazed solemnly up the hills to the sky beyond.

"I'm sorry, girl." He always called me that and I had a sneaking suspicion it was because he couldn't remember my name. "You'll have to cut back a bit. If not, there'll be big problems before the spring rains come."

Cutting back on luxuries was no problem. Cutting back on food was also quite do-able. But cutting back on water? How was that possible? I had one small child and a very small baby still in the early stages of nappy abuse. What's more, I was using the 'terry' type to save both money and unnecessary trips into Richmond, which was seventeen kilometres away.

Consulting Bongile was obviously a necessity. She and her family had lived in a kraal on the farm for generations and had never had access to running water. Every day, one or more members of the family would walk the two or so kilometres across the *veld* to the farmhouse carrying large plastic containers, which they would then fill and hoisting them on their head, walk all the way back. What would they do if I didn't cut down myself?

Finding Bongile in the comfortable stone flagged kitchen of the main house, I asked her how her family managed on such tight water rations. She always seemed to be scrupulous about her own hygiene, so I figured they must have a method.

"Water more important than food, Missy Val." This was her own name for me now. "On the kraal we never throw water away." She made a scornful flapping gesture with her hands to show how she felt about it. "We use ev-ery thing," she said, stressing the 'every' heavily.

She explained the system. Firstly, of the water that was not used for drinking, some was used for washing dishes, and then the dirty remains were saved for watering the *mealie* (maize) patch. Then there was the water for cleaning themselves, which then went on to be used for the laundry, and finally ended up in the vegetable patch. This was efficiency. They had lived like this forever. I felt guilty about my own wastefulness, ashamed at the way I had cheerfully emptied baths, sinks and buckets with no thought as to where the water was coming from.

I had often caught sight of Bongile on the back veranda as she carefully 'strip' washed herself every morning from a bucket, removing and replacing articles of clothing as she finished a part of herself. Maybe we would be doing this soon too, and we would just have to get used to it. It might not seem quite so bad if we could make something of a ritual of it.

I started off with the children, and in place of filling the bathtub, I found a galvanised tin bath and placed it on a towel on the kitchen floor. It only took a couple of buckets to fill it, and my little daughters thought it huge fun as they sat one at each end and splashed each other amid squeals of delight.

Once they were out and towelled off, I added a bit more hot water and used it for myself, squatting down and sponging myself down thoroughly. If I needed to wash my hair, I'd do that first before the children got in. Finally, taking my cue from Bongile, I looked around for a final useful destination for the water. The flowering plants didn't need it in the winter. It never rained then anyway. The only use I could see for it was the lemon bush outside the kitchen door.

Lemons in South Africa ripen late in the season. The new crop was already retarded from lack of rain and still quite small and green when I started depositing the contents of our bath water on its roots. You could almost see the bush relaxing with relief at the pleasure of having a good soaking.

Within a week, we could see a significant change. The fruit began to swell. After a month, the lemon bush became a 'tourist' attraction. Friends were invited to come and see its amazing development. We would stand around it with beers, chatting amiably about the qualities of each individual fruit, cupping them gently in our hands to test their firmness and substance, and nodding at each other knowingly. By August, with the continuous days of warm sunshine, the lemons had grown and ripened to the size of small yellow rugby balls, and the tree was practically groaning under the weight of its own load.

When the Ellenses returned from their extended trip overseas, they were astounded by two striking contrasts. The first was the parched, dry and cracked appearance of their beloved, normally lush Natal; the second was the almost obscene health and wealth of their solitary lemon tree. Never, they said, had they seen it so heavy with fruit of such quality.

The spin-off benefits were divine. We made homemade lemon squash, homemade lemon curd and homemade lemon concentrate. We used lemon juice with almost decadent abandon in cooking and as garnish and thought smugly of the ridiculous prices we'd had to pay for a single solitary fruit back in the UK.

So much, I thought, for the idea that plants and fruit need fresh water to flourish. This lemon tree had seemed to thrive on what was essentially seriously polluted water. I started to look out of the window at night to check whether it was glowing in the dark from all the soap chemicals it had absorbed, but no, it just stood serenely in the moonlight, a contented testament to the unaccustomed care and interest it had received as a result of the drought.

The dry weather persisted into the spring months of September and October, which would normally be the beginning of the rainy season, and despite our careful savings, there came the day when there was just no water left in the tanks.

Ouma and Oupa Ellens were back in residence by this time, so we had a council of war to decide what we were going to do.

There was still plenty of water in the dams, but there was nothing coming in or out, and we had no borehole on the farm. It would have been difficult to know where to sink one anyway as being so far up the mountain, the water table had probably sunk below the depth that would be practicable for drilling. Not only that, it was also extremely expensive.

There was only one thing for it. We would have to actively fetch water from the dams for the two households and fill our tanks manually.

Despite, his advancing years and diminutive height, Willem Ellens was still active and strong, and assumed the role of Commander-in-chief of operations with unaffected ease. I understood he had been with the British RAF during the war, and had also been active in the Dutch resistance, so co-ordinating this kind of activity was like donning an old coat. And indeed, he organised Operation Tank-up with military precision.

A long ladder was set against the side of the water tank, reaching to the top. Bill and I were instructed to be on duty to hoist water containers up to the tank by means of a pulley fixed to the top of the ladder, and empty them in. A troop consisting of Kheswa, his son David and the gardener, Jacob, were stationed at the dam with about fifty jerry cans which they had to fill. In the meantime, one of them helped Oupa Ellens to load up the back of the old Datsun *bakkie* with as many full cans as it would bear, and he would bump his way across the fields back to the house where we off loaded them and started filling while he drove back for another load.

I stood at the foot of the ladder and pulled on the rope to support Bill who was holding the twenty litre cans as he climbed up the ladder. It was all a bit precarious, and my heart was lodged permanently in my stomach as I watched and pulled, but it all went quite smoothly.

In any event, our commander would not have tolerated any show of queasiness or nerves. I imagine when you have thrown yourself out of low flying aircraft in enemy territory as a routine event, a simple activity like climbing a ladder would not impress you as much of a challenge.

Pauline Ellens acted as caterer and provided all the troops with long glasses of lemon squash and delicious flapjacks made from oat flakes, brown flour and treacle accompanied by her warm, gently scolding humour. She was naturally concerned for her tenant's safety, and stood with me issuing scornful, but clearly anxious comments on Bill's fumblings softened by the irrepressible laugh in her voice.

It took the best part of a long morning to fill our tank, and then we had to start again on the even bigger one for the main house. By the end of the day, we were all hot, dirty and very tired, but at least we all had water for another couple of weeks, or even months if we were careful.

We had to be very diligent about boiling every drop we drank, and I filled endless bottles to cool off and keep in the fridge. The children became quite used to drinking bottled water and forgot that in the towns and cities, you could drink from the tap. As a result, when we went to visit their friends, the other children's parents were naturally rather disconcerted by my offspring's sophisticated tastes.

With the spring, the drought also raised the problem of the garden. Oupa Ellens was a keen ornamental gardener, and an even more passionate vegetable gardener.

His vegetable patch looked like a miniature version of the Dutch countryside, as he had carefully constructed little drainage channels between the mini dykes he used for planting his seeds and young plants in. He spent hours in his vegetable patch, and the results were always magnificent, but of course they needed water.

It fell to Jacob, the gardener, to take care of the daily dousing the garden needed, and Oupa always ensured there were plenty of full containers from the dam for him to replenish his watering can.

Nevertheless, it was only just enough, and I had my own plants that also needed a drink every day. I also had a number of pots clustered around the back door onto our veranda, most of which had geraniums in them but a few were still empty, awaiting the day we could afford the water to fill them.

I tried to save a little of our wastewater every day to give to my own plants and so far they had survived quite well, so I was rather pleased. However, I didn't want to let a day go by without giving them something, so when on one occasion I found I had to be away for an afternoon with the girls, I asked Jacob if he wouldn't mind doing the honours for me, and to water the pots on the veranda.

Jacob was quite unlike Kheswa, who brimmed with bright intelligence. It wasn't that he was stupid, as he was very knowledgeable about the garden and the plants, and I often saw Oupa Ellens discussing his horticultural plans with his trusted gardener. However, he was rather unimaginative and tended to take things literally.

Arriving back home rather earlier than I expected, I went in search of Jacob to tell him I could do my own watering, but found I was too late. There he was, complete with his watering can, busily pouring my precious wastewater on the pots – the empty pots. To give him credit, he had soaked the plants first, but when I asked him in blustering disbelief what he was doing, he looked at me in some surprise and said, "But Mama, you say me to water the pots, and I just do what you tell me."

He was right, of course. I had told him to do exactly that, so indeed, what could I say? Nevertheless, it taught me a very salutary lesson about the importance of making my intentions clear, especially when it meant 'spending' our scarce supply of liquid gold.

The drought did break temporarily that year, and did so in somewhat dramatic style.

It was the end of October, which is typically when spring eases seamlessly into summer. However, this spring, the air was so dry and the land so dehydrated that everything was crackling with electricity. Our hair sparked when we brushed it and tried to cling to the hairbrush in a rush of bristling static. We got shocks off everything, even each other. The children no longer wanted goodnight kisses because the sting from my lips frightened them.

It was verging on intolerable, but then one morning, I went out into the garden and was immediately aware of a change in the air. I could smell it. The Drakensberg mountains, which we could normally see so clearly in the distance, were shrouded in clouds. There was a freshness to the atmosphere and the scent of rain, but I knew from past experience this could be deceptive. Bongile was hanging out some washing and came over to stand beside me as I gazed into the distance.

"The rain will come today," she said simply.

"How can you be so sure, Bongile?" I was looking for reassurance, tired of the endless drought. The fun of making every drop of water count was wearing a bit thin, and I longed for a real bath to wallow in.

She sniffed at the air. "I feel it, Missy Val. First, we will have the big noise and then the rain."

I presumed that by 'the big noise' she meant thunder, and indeed, the charged feeling of the atmosphere was a typical sign that an electrical storm was on the way. Nevertheless, this didn't always mean that rain would follow, so I was deliberately sceptical, not wishing to build up my hopes only to have them dashed again.

Then joy of joy, around mid-day, I heard the first rumbles of thunder, and looked out to see the clouds approaching, ominously dark with the telltale vertical grey streaks shooting straight down to the earth, confirming that it was raining quite heavily about twenty kilometres away.

In great excitement, I dashed in to call Ouma Ellens and Bongile out to gaze at this wonderful sight. The three of us stood in the garden and watched the looming clouds with silly grins on our faces. I feel quite convinced that never had the onset of 'bad' weather been greeted with more enthusiasm than it was that day.

The thunder continued to escalate in volume, until an hour or so later it was crashing round us like an invisible demolition squad. I had become more or less immured to African storms by that time, but even so, this one was beginning to unsettle me. Then, the lightening struck. I watched as a livid blue–white streak seared into the grass outside the open kitchen door, followed by an almighty crash that sent little Jojo rushing to the door to watch. The children were totally unaffected by such storms and in fact, seemed to enjoy the commotion, especially baby Mo, who sat in my arms and laughed at the noise going on around us. Feeling that somehow it would be safer to stay put under our corrugated iron roof, we withdrew into the lounge of the cottage and I settled the girls by the window to watch the great event of the breaking drought. As I did so, another flash lit the sky, and to my horror, I saw another blue-white streak, but it wasn't outside. This time it was arcing across the kitchen in the exact place where we had been standing only seconds before.

It seemed that although we had no connection to an electricity supply, the fact that there was wiring in the cottage, installed for use when the Ellenses had had a generator, was sufficient for the lightning to find it an ideal conduit.

Feeling weak with a mixture of shock and relief, I sat with the girls by the window, thanking everything that came to mind for our escape. It was at that moment that I also remembered I had left my own washing on the line outside our back door.

After depositing two small and protesting infants in their bedroom where I thought they would be safest, I ran outside to collect the clothes off the line. My biggest fear was being struck by a bolt of lightning, so I dragged everything off the pegs as rapidly as possible, without really noticing what was going on around me.

Turning round to return to the cottage, I was totally unprepared to be hit by a solid curtain of water. The rain had arrived and in such force that it felt as if I had literally walked into a wall. Within the seconds it took to run the five or so metres from the washing line to the door, I was soaked to the skin. I had never seen such a downpour. It came in absolute torrents and battered our tin roof so hard I couldn't hear anything the children said.

Bongile was right in her prediction, but she had somewhat understated the case. Within half an hour, the dams were full again, the streams were running fiercely and the road outside the gate was flooded. We stood at the window watching in undisguised awe.

When after an hour, the storm had eased off somewhat, I took the children, one in my arm and the other by the hand and we ran out into the garden, laughing and dancing for the sheer joy of being wet from real rain. Bongile joined us and splashed around in the puddles with Jojo like the youngster she really was, while the Ellenses watched us indulgently from the protection of the veranda.

The following twelve months were also marked by their low rainfall, and the drought continued, but for the time being, we'd had a reprieve, and our water restrictions were lifted. That night, we all had long luxurious baths, and became ridiculously excited about even the simple act of flushing the toilet without guilt. Within a few months, however, we were back to water rationing again, but by that time I had learned my lesson. I never took the free flow of water through the taps for granted again.

CHAPTER 4

Sisters In Service

Anyone who has watched the films Zulu or Zulu Dawn will have seen the inhabitants of Natal as a war-like people capable of great bravery and nobility alongside their capacity for both cruelty and rigid discipline.

Of course these stories have to be taken in the context of their time and the conditions prevailing in those far off days, not to mention the inclusion of a good dose of fantasy essential to a block-buster movie.

However, the Zulus, who regard Natal as their own kingdom complete with royal monarch, princes and princesses, still have a strong culture, and the rural areas are the home of these historically proud people who migrated south, rather than being imported, as many of the rest of us were. These days, the Zulu nation is still in the majority across the length and breadth of the region, and although their culture has been somewhat diluted by the delights of convenience living, it is still a force to be reckoned with on a local level.

As in most agricultural areas of South Africa in the 1980's, the big farms were generally owned by people of British or Afrikaans origin. In the Natal midlands it was also customary for the Zulu families who worked on the farms to have their kraals on the same land that employed and supported them. This is largely still the case today, although I believe the arrangements are more formalised, given the depressing current perception that bureaucracy equals progress.

Kheswa and his family had lived on Cottingham at least as long as Willem and Pauline Ellens had owned it, and when they sold out to Tony, the Kheswa clan retained their right to live on the farm as a condition of the sale. However, the family was extensive, and I never really knew how many children there were, because they didn't seem to know how to express their relationships in English. It was obviously easier to say that everyone was either a cousin or a sibling, even if they were simply in-laws.

Bongile, or Bongi as I soon found she preferred to be called, had worked for the Ellenses since she was about twelve years old. Things were already changing by the time I arrived, but when she was a child, it wasn't compulsory for farm children to attend formal schools until the age of fifteen or sixteen, as is the case in Europe, and being a daughter in a large family meant she had to earn her way just like the boys. However, Pauline Ellens had ensured that the child received an education as well as training, and Bongi could read, write and do basic arithmetic. Admittedly, this wasn't exactly preparation for academia, but it was more than many of her contemporaries could do.

On the other hand, she knew more about domestic skills than I have ever learned, and could cook like a dream. At twenty-one, Bongi was a success in her own world, as she had confidence, knowledge and skills. Not only that, she had a good job and the complete trust of her employers. Not a bad achievement for anyone in her society at that time.

Bongi was also wonderful with the children, and adopted them as her charges from day one. On the first morning of our residence in the cottage, I was trying to cope with a squalling baby and a truculent two-year-old simultaneously, and the commotion was such that Bongi came to see what was going on. With the wisdom of someone twice her age, coupled to a figure perfectly designed to provide comfort to small things, she scooped up baby Mo and took her off. The next thing I saw was my recently squalling infant wrapped in a shawl tied round Bongi's back. Fast asleep. Bliss.

From then on, this would happen nearly every day, and Bongi would go about her chores seemingly unaffected by the roughly five kilograms of baby hanging on her back. For her part, Mo was never more at peace than when tied tightly to Bongi's ample warmth, and I often wondered whether there was some primeval force at work here because the towns and villages thronged with mothers bearing similar snoozing burdens.

As for young Jojo, she also adored Bongi, and would spend hours following her around with a feather duster, pretending to help with the housework. I decided later on that she must have been exposed to household chores far too early as I'm convinced that she suffered a burnout at around the age of six. In later years, she seemed to have developed an unfathomable allergic reaction to housework of any sort.

Bongi also encouraged Jojo to adopt the local diet, and she soon learned to love pap (a porridge made from maize). Every morning she would disappear into the kitchen of the farmhouse and come out carrying a bowl of what looked to me like totally unpalatable mush, and gobble it up eagerly. She also helped in the making of the gorgeous soda bread that Bongi made. This was a combination of maize meal and white bread flour, which was mixed with milk, water, a little fat and a good dose of baking soda and then kneaded into a dough. After rolling it all into a smooth round ball, Bongi would wrap the dough in a muslin cloth and boil it for about an hour until a heavenly moist, rich textured bread was produced – mouth watering with the fresh butter made from the farm milk.

I tried my hand at making butter myself, and was so pleased with the results, that I continued to make it throughout the three years we spent on the farm. It is surprisingly easy, but a bit tedious. You simply keep beating cream until it has passed the point of being whipped, and starts to separate from its own water. At that point you keep beating (or churning) until all the liquid is extracted and you are left with the solid, pure butter. The watery remains are a light buttermilk which my children also loved to drink.

Another of Bongi's daily chores was to whip a bowl of cream for Oupa Ellens, which he spooned onto everything without any apparent ill effect, much to my astonishment and his wife's 'tut tutting' disapproval. Then, a second bowl of cream would be beaten into butter which Oupa Ellens also spread on everything with equal lack of consequence. I would have hated to be an artery in his circulatory system though, and had images of his veins cringing as they spotted yet another cholesterol loaded mouthful coming down the hatch.

What made all these foods so immensely satisfying, though, was that they largely came from our own produce. The pleasure of eating homemade bread with farm butter and lemon curd produced from our own fruit was something I have long since treasured, and it was mostly Bongi who taught us how to make them. She had the domestic and cooking skills worthy of Mrs Beaton of the great cookbook fame. I often teased her about this, a compliment she received with a shy twist of her head and a warm shoulder-shaking chuckle of denial.

One day in the early spring of our first year on the farm, Bongi came to my door with a young woman whom she introduced to me as her sister, May. I had my doubts about this sibling relationship as May looked absolutely nothing like her sister at all.

She was a glamorous, fine-boned stunner with rather lighter skin tones than Bongi's and long elegant legs. She was also very smartly dressed in a short pencil skirt and white blouse with ruffles round the neck and wrists. Having gone through the normal pleasantries, I looked to Bongi for help. Why had she brought this beautiful girl to meet me?

"May looking for work, Missy Val. She want to work for you." She pronounced the word 'work' as 'wek', so it took me a moment's mental word processing to realise that she was actually asking for a job.

May obviously noticed my hesitation and misinterpreted it as a reluctance to consider her application. She turned away, but by now I had realised the intention and was rather impressed she had dressed up so smartly to plead her case.

"No, May, don't go," I said, "what kind of work are you looking for?"

"May want to clean house and care for the children," explained Bongi, who had clearly decided she was to be May's spokesperson.

Although everyone I knew in the area had at least one home helper, it had never occurred to me that I should have a maid myself. I was still conditioned by my English upbringing into believing it wasn't necessary, and indeed that was true really. I wasn't working yet, so I had more than enough time to do the household chores, and still be able to visit friends and neighbours in the valley.

However, I also knew that it was the only form of employment most of the young women in the area were likely to get, as with the limits of their education, they were not equipped to work in offices and other businesses. It was a tragic fact of life for the majority of them, so in some ways, I could see it was also my duty to employ a girl from Kheswa's family as I was now living on 'their' farm.

I invited May into the kitchen, and taking this as a signal that she had completed her part of the negotiations, Bongi left us to it. The problem was that May didn't speak any English at all, so we had to communicate by sign language. This went quite well until it came to the matter of her wages. I had demonstrated the cleaning tasks by acting out the parts, but didn't know how to ask her what she expected to earn. I tried writing down the numbers to see if this would help, as she certainly knew how to count and what the Rand symbol meant, but seemed uncertain as to what I was suggesting.

Eventually, I took my purse out of my bag, and using my fingers as counters and a small heap of notes and coins, we negotiated an amount of twenty Rands per month. It seemed pitifully little to me, although the Rand was worth much more then than it is today, but even still, it was hardly a living wage. Nevertheless, she seemed quite adamant that that was what she wanted.

When I queried this with Gwen, she assured me that this was the going rate for a housemaid, and that Bongi probably didn't earn much more, if anything. Seeing that I was still troubled, she went on further to say that I should bear in mind May's overall situation. She lived on the farm, so she paid no rent; her father worked for the Ellenses, as did Bongi and David, meaning they all received food rations as well as their wages; she didn't have overheads such as electricity and phone bills, so in the end, the money she earned was probably hers to spend as she saw fit.

Given, too, that the shops the locals frequented were considerably cheaper than our supermarkets, it wasn't as bad as it appeared. Lastly, and most importantly, there was a kind of honour among both the farmers and their workers in that no one was paid more or less than the accepted rate for the job they did. That would have caused friction and possibly even open conflict. How the accepted rate was arrived at, I was never to find out, but the standard was there, and May knew better than to expect me to contradict it.

In fact, on one occasion, Tony the farmer told me he had decided to give his own workers a pay rise, which would have increased their wages to above the standard rate. Apparently his intentions were purely economic. He thought the absentee rate would go down and that they would put in more effort if they were better paid. On the contrary, although his employees all gratefully accepted the extra cash when he handed them their pay at the end of the month, his plan backfired when none of them turned up for work the following day. I think he was still nonplussed about it even when he told me, but had been forced to accept the fact that his employees felt they had been paid too much, and so didn't need to work for the next few days.

May started work the day after her interview, arriving at eight in the morning. Curiously, though, I noticed she was once again dressed very glamorously considering she was about to don a housecoat and start cleaning floors. Still, she got to work willingly enough, and by ten o'clock, she had done most of the housework. At that point, she took her mug of tea and plate of bread and jam out into the garden to join Bongi for her morning break.

Jodie also joined them and chattered away like a happy sparrow to the two sisters. Bongi then transferred baby Mo from her back to May's as a signal that it was now her job to look after my baby who obligingly continued sleeping without a stir.

For the rest of the morning, May's job was to watch over Jojo and Mo, so she stayed out in the garden talking kiddy Zulu to them and playing with them until one o'clock when she took off her housecoat and dressing once again in her elegant attire, she went home.

The following days followed a similar pattern, which then turned into the following weeks. However, as time went by, I couldn't help noticing another pattern forming. On certain days of the week, May would appear dressed as if for a nightclub and usually about half an hour late. This didn't really concern me, except that gradually I noticed that on these particular mornings she seemed to be more than usually tired, yawning almost constantly. I was also fascinated to see that the children took to yawning with her in sympathy

Her attention to the housework diminished accordingly, and she spent almost all her time acting as nanny to the children. Again, I let it go, and didn't worry about it too much. She did at least keep Jojo amused, and looked after Mo diligently, changing her nappies when needed and carrying her everywhere to the point that I was worried my child would never learn to walk.

Then one day, May arrived wearing the mini-est of mini dresses in red satin, smelling of a mixture of perfume and alcohol, and looking as if she hadn't slept a wink. Feeling that this did not augur well for our future relationship, I called Bongi and asked her to interpret for me while I quizzed May about what was going on.

Both Bongi and May looked distinctly shamefaced, and muttered quickly to each other out of the corners of their mouths. There was a shrug from May, and a hiss from Bongi, and then it seemed that they had agreed to come clean because when Bongi spoke, she did so without looking at me and with a studied neutrality of expression.

"Missy Val, May have another job. She work nights. She earn very much at night."

The penny dropped. Those few words, together with the total absence of expression on Bongi's face, made me realise just what kind of work we were talking about. I had employed a 'lady of the night'. A very beautiful, elegant lady of the night to be sure, but I felt this was hardly a good combination with her day job as a nanny. What I couldn't understand was why, under the circumstances, she felt she needed another job at all.

Bongi provided the explanation. Kheswa didn't know what May did, as she always made sure he never saw her dressed up for 'work', and it was Kheswa who wanted May to take a job with me. The fact that she was often not home at night must have been questioned, but I didn't take it any further. I didn't really want to know as I wasn't sure how complicated the deception might be. What I did make clear to both these girls was that May had to come to a decision. She could either work for me, or she could continue with her night-time 'job', but not both. I finished by saying she could go home now, think it over, and let me have her decision the next day

I left them with all the stern dignity I could muster, and was highly entertained to see them throwing whispered abuse at each other in the garden before May threw off her housecoat, grabbed her bag and stomped off looking for all the world as if her sister had fired her.

As I had expected, she didn't turn up to work the next day. Or the next. In the light of the decision she had to make, and the pros and cons of each choice, I guessed she felt that, on balance, she was better off with her night job. It was certainly more lucrative, and the standard rate was probably higher anyway. I only wished I could have made it more attractive for her to work days, but I doubt if I could have got away with thumbing my nose at such an entrenched system.

Following May's departure, life more or less went back to normal, and Mo resumed her position on Bongi's back as if settling back into a comfy old chair. One day a few months later, Bongi came to me and asked if I minded if she took the children home with her that afternoon. There were several small 'brothers and sisters' on the kraal that Jojo would enjoy playing with.

Slightly surprised and a little hesitant, I agreed but asked her to promise to bring them back before five, and then, throwing caution to the winds watched her walking briskly off the farm, holding Jojo firmly by the hand with Mo in her usual place at the rear.

The kraal was about two kilometres away, and was reached by a well-worn pathway across the *veld*. I had only been there a couple of times, and even then not right to the kraal itself. There was another even older settlement on route which had long since been deserted, and Bill liked to go there occasionally to practise target shooting at the collection of old cans that had been left behind. As a result, I more or less knew where she was going, and I just trusted to Bongi's obvious devotion to my children that she wouldn't let them come to any harm. Although there were snakes everywhere, the path was so well beaten and the Kheswa clan so experienced that I had no qualms about that, but there were always thorns, insects and possibly broken glass to worry about. I decided not to worry.

Fortunately, the threesome returned on time, shortly before five that afternoon, and I experienced a release of tension that I hadn't even realised I was feeling. However, taking hold of Jojo's hand, I was struck by the strong and pungent smell emanating from my exuberantly happy three-year old. I couldn't place it, and to my unaccustomed nostrils, it was awful. It was as if something had died and she'd rolled in it, and then taken another roll in the ashes of a recently extinguished wood fire.

I wasn't too far out as it happened, as except for the rotting corpse, my impression was pretty close to the truth. I learned from my excited child that she'd had a lovely time and played with all the children; she'd also helped make the *phutu* (a development of *pap* that contained less water and was more like mashed potato). This involved sitting close to the wood fire and being cuddled by Bongi's mother, who liked to smear herself with chicken grease to prevent dry skin problems. The combination of the grease and the wood smoke was what gave off the rather sickly, acrid stench that seemed to permeate everything my daughter was wearing.

What amazed me was that Bongi herself never smelt like this, but this was because she was, as she told me solemnly, a modern young woman. She used patented preparations bought from the shops, rather than the chicken or animal fat her mother continued to use. She also changed her clothes as soon as she arrived at the farm, as Ouma Ellens had taught her early on to wash and change as a matter of routine.

What was even more surprising was that she didn't seem to notice the children had picked up and absorbed the smoke and grease fumes that she herself worked so hard to avoid.

Jojo seemed totally oblivious of the reeking aura she now possessed, but made no objection to being bathed and scrubbed from top to toe, prattling away continuously about how much she had enjoyed her afternoon. She had eaten *phutu* with her hands, and played around in the dust with the other children, stripping off as many of her clothes as possible to be like them.

I didn't have it in my heart to forbid any further adventures to the kraal - it was so much fun for Jojo to have so many other children to play with. But I have to confess I didn't actively encourage it. On the occasions when they did go, I had the bath prepared and ready for the moment they arrived home. I could then pick them up and lower them into the water while holding my breath, so that I wouldn't have to inhale the unadulterated smells of a rather earthier existence.

After May left me, I didn't see her that often, as she moved to Edendale. She did come home on occasions to be with her family, but whether they knew about her chosen career was never made clear. When I sometimes saw her with Bongi, she seemed cheerful enough, so I had to assume all was well.

Nevertheless, one occasion when the two sisters were seen together stood out in all our memories, although I only heard about it later from Bill who was actively, if rather reluctantly, involved.

Every year Pietermaritzburg is home to the Royal Show, the most important agricultural exhibition in the province. It is a grand and important event, and anticipated eagerly by everyone in the area. There are cattle judging contests, agricultural machinery displays, stalls selling local produce and vegetables and a tent for all the home industries fostered by the Women's Institute. There are equestrian events, dog shows and every other conceivable contest or competition associated with rural and agricultural life. Added to that, there is always a display of Zulu dancing, and hundreds of young Zulu maidens and youths turn up, dressed in full traditional costume, to perform.

The show lasts about ten days, and includes two weekends. In the early 1980's it was as popular as ever, and given the nature of Bill's job as an automotive paint expert, he was on duty at his company's display tent every day of the show, including both weekends.

On the first Saturday of the show that particular year, he was leaving the farm in his company car, a smart red Ford Escort, when he spotted Bongi and May on the dirt road up ahead. Both of them were dressed as traditional Zulu maidens, meaning they were not wearing anything on their upper bodies except necklaces of elaborate beadwork. For the rest, they were garbed in the typical beaded skirts and headdresses befitting daughters of the proud culture from which they had come.

Highly amused at seeing the girls dancing and singing their way along the road, Bill stopped to ask them where they were off to, thinking they were heading for a local wedding or other celebration.

To his shock and embarrassment, they immediately hopped in the back of the car, clearly believing he had stopped to give them a lift, and announced they were going to the Royal Show. Bill then had no choice but to drive the entire distance to the show, as well as into the showground itself, with two ample bosomed beauties for passengers, beauties who clearly took great delight in having their own personal chauffeur.

Getting out of the car, they each gave him a smacking kiss on the cheek, mischievously aware of the stir they were causing amongst Bill's team, all of whom were young Zulu men. Bill tried somewhat sheepishly to explain who the girls were, but quickly gave up when he saw the look of disbelief on the faces of his crew. However, his embarrassment turned to rather smug pride when he finally realised that far from being shocked, or even critical, the young men were regarding him with a new respect. The boss didn't just have a wife at home, but he also had not just one, but two gorgeous girlfriends. Not bad for an *omdala* (old guy).

CHAPTER 5

Friends, Animals And Countryman

Hollanders Forever

Willem and Paulien Ellens, our neighbours, mentors and landlords on the farm, were never referred to as being 'Dutch'. They were Hollanders, the reason being that to be branded a 'Dutchman' in Natal was definitely not a compliment and was associated with *boers* or *skaaps* both of which were derogatory terms for people of Dutch South African origin you didn't like. By the same token, people of British origin were known as *rooieneks*. It was thus very important to distinguish recent imports like the Ellenses from the home-grown descendants of their forbears by clarifying their nationality in this way.

What I didn't really appreciate for some time after we moved to the farm was how very 'Hollandish' they still were, despite the long years they had spent in South Africa. It was always interesting to listen to them speaking to each other because they would switch languages half way through a conversation or even a sentence without noticing. This presented no problem to them, of course, but if anyone else was involved in the discussion, it became somewhat disconcerting. It was rather like switching radio channels from an English to a foreign station without giving any explanation.

African Ways

Oupa Willem's English was very good and extremely correct. He spoke slowly and deliberately, pronouncing each word as if he'd tested it beforehand, and he rarely, if ever, used slang or substituted Dutch words for English. Ouma Paulien, on the other hand, peppered her speech with anglicised *Nederlands* and shamelessly used every South African cliché in the book.

Before I had ever ventured out of oh-so-English Natal, I had learnt that a dinger was not a bell or something that went 'ding'; it was an Ouma word for a thing, derived from the Dutch '*ding, dingen*'. This became highly amusing when she wanted to bake something in the oven. She had a timer that 'dinged' at the end of the allotted cooking period, and I heard her tell Bongi on more than one occasion to put the 'dinger on with the dinger'.

I also learnt the word *lekker*, which means not just tasty as it does in Dutch, but anything, including the weather, that was nice, and that *veld* was the Dutch (and South African) word for open fields. She talked about things being 'finished and *klaar*' two words which mean the same thing, but to use both was to emphasise the completion. Then if something was *door mekaar*, it was in a hopeless muddle.

It took me some time to work out what all these puzzling expressions meant, and oddly, it never occurred to me that she was using vocabulary from her own language. I simply accepted them as 'Ouma speak'.

The Ellenses also remained very Dutch in their home customs. Ouma had brought all her traditional ideas about house keeping with her to her adoptive country, and she managed to make each task a small ritual. She had the most beautiful carved and inlaid Dutch, oak wardrobe with a deep, moulded cornice at the top and ball-shaped feet. She cherished this piece and once a year, after preparing a special beeswax polish, she would spend the whole day cleaning and applying a new coat of wax to every nook and cranny of its complex panels.

Then there was the way in which she taught Bongi to starch and press all her linen, which was always blindingly white due to the hours it spent drying in the brilliant sunshine. I loved the smells and scents of her home produced floor polish and fresh flowers, her soaps and newly ironed cottons. It always made me feel that keeping house at this level was a real vocation, even maybe an art form.

Considering her infirmity, Paulien Ellens was always cheerfully resourceful, and let nothing prevent her from leading a life that would have left many a younger, fitter soul fading behind her. She was a leading light in the local Women's Institute, giving advice and talks on a variety of skills and crafts. She was equally fund raiser and hell raiser for the Pietermaritzburg Rotary Club. She also went to the Lions Club and did hospital visits even when she could barely walk herself. Then for relaxation, she spent hours under the soft glow from the oil lamps embroidering exquisite tray cloths and towels. In short, she was hardly ever to be found without some form of planning or activity to keep her busy mind occupied. I was filled with both deep affection and amazed awe for this courageous, elderly Dutch matriarch.

As for Oupa, in company with all good 'Hollanders', his life revolved around his yacht; his real magnum opus. The fact that there are more boats per capita in the Netherlands than anywhere else in the world is merely a testament to the importance these people of the Low Countries attach to their water sports. So, never mind the fact that the farmhouse was close to the top of a mountain, or that the nearest dam large enough for water sports was roughly sixty kilometres distant, Willem Ellens had to have his yacht, which he was intent on building himself.

When we arrived on the farm, we noticed the framework of a catamaran on one of the verandas at the side of the house. It was carefully covered over, so we couldn't see how far it had progressed, but when the Ellenses arrived back from their long overseas trip, almost the first thing old Willem did was to peel off the dust sheets and protective plastic so that he could resume his life's work.

It was difficult to foresee a time when he would be able to sail it. Willem Ellens was well into his seventies when I met him, as was his wife. His yacht was an impeccably crafted frame at that moment, built entirely with hand tools (no electricity available). It had taken him several years to reach this stage. Given that the first skin of the boat was made using individual strips of ply wood about five centimetres wide, maybe even less, my totally non mathematical mind couldn't cope with any kind of calculation on the probable length of time it would take to complete it, but I knew it had to be years.

I tried to imagine an eighty somethinger with a somewhat disabled wife launching a twelve-metre catamaran – and failed. What I did admire tremendously, though, was his painstaking attention to detail and perfect craftsmanship, not to mention the sheer dogged tenacity of his determination to finish it and go sailing. Mental images of Willem as a terrier with a bone came rather easily to mind.

Considering his somewhat taciturn nature, what also surprised me was his grandfatherly tolerance for an unanticipated adoptive grand daughter. In truth, he had a heart of gold, but we adults only had occasional glimpses of his deep well of human kindness. Jojo, however, experienced it on a daily basis. She used to take her mug of tea, sometimes even her bowl of *pap*, and go to the veranda every morning to watch him while he worked.

Sitting on a bench with her legs swinging, Jojo prattled away to her Oupa asking endless annoying and pointless questions – as children do – and he would either answer her or ignore her as he saw fit, just working on with his boat. As far as I know, he never, ever told her to go away.

Jojo also trotted around after him when he was working in the vegetable garden or seeing to the farm animals, and her childish candour only floored him once. Holding his hand one morning as they did a tour of inspection, my small daughter noticed a bull mounting one of the cows in a nearby paddock.

"Oh, look Oupa!" the innocent toddler pointed to the coupling cattle, "What's that bully doing? His big willy's all hanging out!"

Poor Willem. He just couldn't cope with this. At seventy-seven, he really wasn't equipped to tell small girls about the 'facts of life', the birds, the bees or anything else. Blushing scarlet, so Pauline told me later in great amusement, he suggested that she should come and ask me, but Jojo was not to be diverted.

"Mum doesn't know anything about bully beefs, Oupa. You're the farmer."

Almost crippled with embarrassment by now, Willem made some lame excuse about the bull just 'playing' with the cow, but with that insight that children so often have, Jojo knew he was hiding something. She also knew instinctively that she wouldn't extract anything more from him on the subject and so, later that day, I found myself giving my four-year old her first instruction in the mysteries of procreation.

The explanation was predictably met with disbelieving giggles and hilarity, and I tend to think that Jojo believed Oupa's explanation rather more readily than the unlikely truth of mine. I suppose when described in purely technical terms, the act of mating does sound rather absurd and inefficient. Even baby-carrying storks must seem more plausible than the real thing to a small child.

During a nostalgic visit back to Natal in the nineties, I learned that Willem Ellens did eventually finish his yacht some several years after I left the farm. He even sailed it once with the help of his entire family. But sadly, he was never strong enough to make the journey of his dreams up the coast of Africa to Zanzibar.

Nevertheless, I firmly believe that the great yacht-building project was what kept this very dear, elderly gentleman going in his retirement. It seems rather significant that following its completion, he deteriorated rapidly both mentally and physically, and died within the space of just a few years. Not so his wife, who had perhaps more strings to her proverbial bow.

My animals and other family

By spring of our first year on the farm, we already felt as if we belonged there. We had experienced the hottest days of a summer, the magnificence of a Natal Midlands autumn, and the parched dryness of winter. In addition, we had survived the sometimes nerve shattering drama of African weather changes from violent electrical storms to crippling drought, neither of which we had ever experienced in Europe. On the other hand, there were days when we were shrouded in cloud at the top of our mountain, enduring soaking drizzle. Then again, there were the weeks of blistering heat with searing blue skies and endless horizons.

I loved it. I had never been happier. England with its economic hardships made indescribably wretched by cold miserable winters seemed like another lifetime – a distant memory. Even better, we had found truly wonderful surrogate grandparents for our young children in the Ellenses, who were also very dear friends to us older 'children'. We also had the best near neighbour we could wish for in Gwen, who had been our mentor and guide since we first moved in.

She had been a staunch stalwart from the first. I called on her repeatedly during the early days, and her advice was invaluable, especially when dealing with the local Zulus, as she spoke their language fluently and understood their customs and habits in a way that was both sympathetic and realistic. She showed me many useful skills as well, ranging from how to use the farm phone – a wonderfully archaic wind-up affair – to how to remove the menace of blood sucking ticks from the skin with a red-hot match tip or cigarette butt.

Generally speaking, Gwen stood no nonsense and was immensely practical. In contrast, though, she operated at a deeply intuitive level as well. Her knowledge of what we now term alternative remedies was extensive, and she had an awareness of plant and bird life that seemed almost mystical to me. I was intrigued, influenced, charmed and drawn to this slim, almost boyish looking grandmother who seemed to breathe the life of Africa.

The cottage Gwen shared with her husband formerly belonged to the Ellenses, and was a pretty, white-painted chalet that perched on the side of the mountain where it sloped down to meet the road. They had a gorgeous garden filled with bougainvillea, plumbago and climbing geraniums. It also had a lusciously green lawn, but because of its steep angle, its only apparent use was for the children (both her offspring's and mine) to roll down it in interminable tumbling games - a pastime which seemed to carry an obligation to scream and giggle hysterically, all of which Gwen took in her cool, collected stride.

She adored all young things, which was of course reciprocated enthusiastically, and Jojo and Mo loved the afternoons we spent at the cottage. 'Gork', as her grandchildren called her, always had interesting things to look at and play with, and seemed to have a limitless fund of patience to tell stories about her precious collections. There were shells and stones, as well as African bead work and little models, and everything had its own story. With a child on each knee, Gwen told fables of Zulu legend and myth that had my two usually hyperactive infants both enthralled and blissfully quiet for hours at a time.

To add to their delight, especially Mo's, Gwen also had a cat. The Ellenses had three large dogs, all very friendly and good natured, but I imagine that when you are very small yourself, cats are relatively more interesting in terms of cuddle value. Result: Mo was obsessed by Gwen's motley coloured moggy, a female of great character and apparently prolific breeding, for during the first weeks of each spring, she produced a large crop of healthy kittens providing Gwen with the perennial problem of what to do with them.

Following the first birthing of our residence, I was aware that hints were being dropped with the subtlety of a ten ton cannon ball, but I remained determinedly obtuse and blithely ignored Gwen's loaded remarks about my daughters' affection for her feline nursery. I told her firmly and repeatedly that I didn't want to be saddled with any pets until Mo herself was less dependent on me.

During the first spring, this ploy succeeded, despite several assaults on my emotional fortitude. I suppose this was because at that stage, Mo was too young to be vocal about it, and as a result, unable to practise her manipulative skills on either Gwen or me. However, in the second spring, my defence system failed me. Gwen's cat again produced her regulation litter of kittens and naturally, we were called upon to pay our respects to mum and babies alike.

Admittedly, they were adorable. There were six of them, and they were mostly all tabby, with the exception of one that was tortoiseshell and white. They looked like six little wriggling sausages lined up in a neat row as they suckled their proudly purring mother, and I found that even my stubborn determination was vulnerable, although I adamantly refused to admit it - even to myself.

For Mo, it was love at first sight. Now she had found her voice, she pestered me tirelessly and cajoled me unremittingly, but I was not to be moved. What I didn't know, however, was that she was simultaneously working on Gwen, convincing her with all the wiles available to a scheming two-year-old that we needed a cat of our own, and that it was something I really wanted, even when I said I didn't. I might have guessed that resistance was pointless, but I suppose I was reluctant to acknowledge that I could be over-ruled by a daughter who had only recently learnt to speak. Such an admission wouldn't really bode well for my future role as a guiding influence in her life, so it was safer for my self-esteem to pretend otherwise.

Given the odds that were stacked against me, though, I shouldn't have been as surprised as I was one morning when Gwen's husband appeared at my door carrying a tiny tortoiseshell and white handful of fluff with a bunch of claws at each corner, which was yelling indignantly from its disproportionately strong lungs. Handing the resentful bundle into the suspiciously ready arms of my youngest child, he guilelessly informed me that he had brought me my kitten.

It took me a moment to realise he actually wasn't kidding. I was utterly speechless. It appeared to be a fait accompli. Or a brilliant stroke of genius. How could I now be so rude as to blatantly repudiate what clearly seemed to him to be a pre-arranged delivery? I couldn't of course, and I was left with not just the kitten, but the uncomfortable realisation I had been trounced in the first of many battles of will with my little Mo.

Gwen was conspicuous by her absence on this occasion, and I was more than ever convinced that she was fully aware of my ideas on the matter. She knew perfectly well I didn't want another addition to my household. What's more, I couldn't help feeling that it was a well-planned manoeuvre on her part to send a blissfully ignorant envoy in her place. Her husband's innocence was my undoing, but as it turned out, Gwen was right in the end.

The kitten quickly endeared herself to us all, and in place of the exotic African name she arrived with, soon answered to the simple call of Mitten. The girls were only too happy to take care of her and their diligence at house training the poor animal was comical. Never has a cat been shown the garden more frequently and with such enthusiastic instruction to do its duty than that tiny bewildered creature.

Over the weeks following her arrival, and about once an hour during the day, I got used to seeing one or other small person dashing through the kitchen with Mitten clutched unceremoniously under an arm or stretched out in front like the blunt end of a battering ram. The next moment, there followed a peremptory command of "wee Mitten, wee!", with much disgusted sighing and tutting if the poor thing failed to perform. Nonetheless, the rigorous training was a success. Mitten was probably the cleanest, most reliable cat I have ever had, and would have passed muster with the strictest sergeant major.

I should add here that she was even more prolific than her mother and within the next two years, she produced five litters of kittens, falling pregnant on each occasion within six weeks of her previous confinement. The strange thing was that I never saw a candidate for her affections in the area, and none of our immediate neighbours owned to having a Tom. All the same, she found several suitors somewhere, because her litters were marked by their variety and she hardly ever had two babies the same.

Most of our neighbours accepted that cats had unwanted kittens, and were unsentimental about disposing of them by drowning immediately after birth. We were too lily-livered for this, and couldn't bring ourselves to such a level of detachment. So, like Gwen, we resorted to fair means and foul to find homes for our furry burdens. To both my amusement and guilt, I found myself practising flagrant acts of emotional blackmail not only on the children's friends, but also on my own, or their house staff or anyone I could persuade into giving a home to one of my poor 'orphans'. I am both ashamed and proud to say that it worked without fail. Who says you can't teach old dogs new tricks? Or cats, for that matter.

As she grew to maturity, we began to realise that Mitten thought she was a dog; not surprising given that her most frequent companions were Danny, a Bull Mastiff, a Labrador cross called Suzy and an ancient Dobermann with the exalted name of Brutus in keeping with his status as the 'old man' of the pack.

Brutus was really the odd one out because of his great age. He was very much his master's dog, and kept close to Willem Ellens rather than consorting with the other two. Sadly, poor Brutus could no longer bark properly as his voice had deteriorated to a rather wheezy sounding cough. Nevertheless, he tried his best to maintain his dignity by performing when expected, even though the sound he produced was about as threatening as a frog with a sore throat.

As it happened, he felt it was still his duty to round the cows up for milking, and on many occasions I watched him honking hoarsely at them through the fence, hopping up and down on his front legs with the effort. Despite the feebleness of the vocal results, which sometimes expired completely if he'd had an especially busy session, the cows actually responded and did as he bid them. They seemed to know that he was trying to do his job, and obediently lined up at the gate ready to go to the milking shed. Their expressions clearly said, "Poor old codger. Better let him think he's still in charge," just to humour him.

Danny and Suzy, on the other hand, were young, boisterous females, who roared around the garden getting in everyone's way and competing with each other for attention and snacks, or anything else that might involve favours. It took Mitten all of two swipes delivered with a malevolent hiss to bring the pair to order, and thereafter, she cruised round them bossing them about unmercifully.

When we arrived home, Danny and Suzy always came to the gate to greet us. And so did Mitten. When they circled the car, eagerly waiting for us to get out, so did she. While they barked excitedly, tongues lolling and dribbling with glee at seeing us, Mitten yowled and whined, weaving round our legs as we cautiously opened the doors and stepped out.

They became quite a threesome, and whenever I took the two dogs for a walk, Mitten came trotting briskly along too, complaining bitterly but refusing to be left behind. She usually walked quite a distance with us, but she had her territorial boundaries, and when she reached them, she used to turn round and go home, moaning even more vociferously if we didn't follow her.

I never worried when I was out alone with the children and the animals, and always felt perfectly safe. The only possible danger in the area was from snakes and baboons, although I did once see a leopard skirting the side of the mountain, but this was so far off that it presented no threat to us. The baboons mostly kept their distance too, confining themselves to nightly raids on the fruit trees, as on a few occasions I woke during the night to hear the dogs barking furiously at their subversive incursions.

That left the snakes. On the whole, there was little danger there too, as snakes tend to be very shy creatures and as long as they can hear or rather feel the vibration of approaching footsteps, they will make themselves scarce. Mitten often used to bring in the small harmless Herald snakes, which she kindly beheaded and left as gifts for me

76

on the kitchen floor. My first encounter with one of these charming offerings reduced me to a quivering wreck until Jacob, the gardener, assured me they were totally without venom. I then became surprisingly immune to finding the various parts of dismembered reptiles decorating my floors.

So it was that I was quickly lulled into a false sense of security about hazardous wildlife and was totally unsuspecting and unprepared when I did have a more serious confrontation with the local serpentine population.

It happened one day when the girls, the dogs, Mitten and I were taking one of our regular strolls along the dirt road leading towards Gwen's cottage. It had been a particularly cold winter's morning, and I was trying to catch some of the midday sun to take the chill from my bones. The sun was shining brightly, and I had turned my face towards it to feel the warmth soaking into my skin. The world was just beginning to feel like a better place to inhabit when my composure was shattered by an ear splitting shriek from one of my daughters.

Looking down, I froze in mid stride. In front of us on the road was a large Puff Adder coiled loosely with its underside exposed. It too was enjoying the rays of the winter sun, and I was just about disrupt its peace by putting a clumsy great foot squarely in its middle, something I doubt if it would have been too pleased about.

Fortunately, though, we had Mitten with us. The dogs were useless. They scattered like the cowardly beasts they really were, but Mitten was a little trooper. Circling the snake, she hissed and clawed at it until in desperate confusion, the poor thing took off into the bushes with her giving chase. As soon as it had disappeared though, she returned to join us, behaving for all the world as if nothing had happened. While the children and I were still shaking from the near-miss, she simply resumed her customary moaning and complaining.

Weak with relief we turned back and went home, eager to share our traumatic experience with anyone who would listen. Finding Willem at his usual post on the veranda, I told him what had happened, my tale punctuated with exclamations of wild exaggeration from an over-excited Jodie, and supported by Mo who always tried to out shout her sister anyway, come what may.

To our collective disappointment, Willem was not surprised. Pausing from his work, his chiselling temporarily suspended, he explained that snakes also felt the cold and were great sun worshippers. It made sense that during the winter when the ground was generally several degrees cooler than they liked it, the dirt roads were sun spots where they could find some comfort as the sand warmed up faster than the grasslands where they usually hid.

"You will often see snakes in the sunny patches on these country lanes," he said, directing his careful words to two small wide-eyed girls. "Most of the time, they feel the cars coming and rush off the road to safety, but you must have surprised your Puff Adder by walking up on it too quietly. It must have been quite deeply asleep," he finished up. "You were very, very lucky the cat was so brave, or it might have bitten you in fright." He waggled his chisel at us in admonishment, whether for not noticing the snake or for frightening it was not quite clear. The message that was really clear was that, after this incident, I should keep my eyes carefully down when out walking, a habit I haven't really given up even now.

African Ways

Local amenities with a difference

Village post offices in Europe often serve a social as well as a practical function. When I was growing up in the west country of England, the small local post offices did a great deal more than just selling stamps and registering letters. They often sold groceries on a small scale, but mostly they offered sweets, newspapers and cigarettes, and were sometimes the only shop for miles around. This type of combined service was normal in the average rural English community, and there were usually banking facilities as well.

At the post office in Elandskop, Natal, there was no shop, or indeed any other extra apart from the standard post office savings account system. Indeed, the post mistress was far too busy operating the local telephone exchange alongside her postal duties, a job which left her little time between the stamps and the registered mail for anything else.

Nonetheless, a curious common factor about village post offices everywhere is that they nearly always seem to have a maiden-aunt-style middle-aged lady in attendance, and ours was no exception. To me, our post mistress's name was Mavis, because even if it wasn't, it should have been. She was probably married, but didn't look as if she could be, and equally, she may have had children, but her style was so much that of the classic spinster that Mavis has remained so in my memory to this day. More importantly, she was the heart and lungs of our little universe, pumping the life through our communication lines every day of the working week between precisely 10.00 in the morning and 4.30 in the afternoon.

As we had no postal deliveries to the farms, we all had the same address at the post office, which was quite simply PO Box Elandskop 4540 Natal. Each resident had a pigeon hole on one wall of the small post office waiting area, into which Mavis slotted our letters and packages. We then had to go and collect our mail ourselves which was a round trip of about sixteen kilometres. Naturally, we didn't go every day and my relatives were sometimes a little nonplussed when I told them I only got my post once a week. The idea of not having mail delivered to their front door was beyond their comprehension in the late 20th century.

It always amazed me that post from my family thousands of kilometres away in England actually found me by using this incredibly basic address, but it did. Admittedly, it was slow and sometimes came by rather circuitous routes, but most of the time it arrived eventually. I do recall one occasion when a letter my father sent me finally arrived six months later having travelled by way of Cleveland, Ohio. It turned up at PO Box Elandskop a bit battered, slightly travel weary but still in one piece.

The telephones were old fashioned party lines, and given that there were only two lines to cover both the mountain road and the valley, Mavis was kept very busy routing calls to the different homesteads sharing the cable along these two trajectories. Our call signals were defined by our actual numbers; on the farm, we were one-seven-double two, and our code was two short rings and two long ones. Gwen was one-seven-two-one, and so she had two short rings, one long and another short one. On this basis, while we heard the calls for everyone on our line, we were only supposed to answer to our own code. It didn't always work this way, however, as some of us were not quite as adept at using our phones as others.

We could, of course, call anyone on our own line free of charge by ringing the codes ourselves. The telephones themselves had no dials or key pads. They were beautiful old Bakelite instruments consisting of an old-fashioned wedge shaped base, with the normal hand piece on the top for speaking and listening. On the right hand side of the base, there was a handle used for making the calls. This involved turning it furiously round and round for the long rings and then a brief burst for the short rings, but it took some practice. When I first used it, I frequently got the wrong person and often had to apologise while blaming my fumbling incompetence - although I suspected that there were one or two of the neighbours who answered anyway, whoever the call was for.

Mavis, on the other hand, knew everyone personally. In a way, she was the community receptionist, and many of us, farmers and homesteaders alike, used to let her know when we would be out so that she didn't have to waste time trying to connect callers to us. The post office number was one long burst, and to make any call to the outside world, we had to ring Mavis at the exchange and she made the connection for us. By the same token, the rest of the world had to call the exchange first and she would then put them through to the appropriate household.

Of course, we could also just call Mavis, and ask her to divert our calls to someone else, or take messages for us, or simply say we were out if we didn't want to be bothered by the phone for a while. She was terribly efficient in her quiet way, and rarely forgot a request or instruction. Given that she was also busy at the post office counter helping her Zulu customers send their wage packets to their relatives by recorded delivery, as well as sorting the post into the post boxes, she managed her 'secretarial' duties with worthy diligence.

There was one instance while I was waiting my turn at the counter when I watched in fascination as she guided an old African gentleman through the weighty procedure of sending fifty Rands to his daughter in Cape Town, while simultaneously making an international call to Holland for Paulien Ellens. With the receiver hooked behind her left ear and held in place with her chin, she managed to juggle the complexities of explaining postal orders to old Solomon with asking the international exchange to connect her to a number in The Hague.

"The payee is your daughter, Solomon ... yes, operator, I said The Hague in the Netherlands. The number is ... no, Solomon, your daughter's name goes there ... sorry, operator, the number is oh-seven-oh ... that's right ... seven ... good Solomon, now put your ... what was that? Right ... the rest of? Yes, it's ... no, here Solomon, not there...," and so she continued, unflappable, controlled, in charge of her world, and ours for that matter.

But, there was another unexpected dimension to this service. It was the 20th century development on the bush telegraph, and I encountered it somewhat by chance. One day, my sister tried to phone me from the UK. I was out when the call came through, but I had rung Mavis to tell her I would be away for the day. Knowing that I would want to have a message from such a long distance relative, Mavis put the call through to Gwen, who had a nice neighbourly chat with my sister, took down the message, and rung off with the promise to fill me in when I arrived home.

Later that day, I was driving back along the dirt road that skirted our mountain when the housemaid from the next farm along the road waved me to a halt.

"Ah, mama," she started excitedly, "you go home fast, now. You see Madam Gwen. She have important message for you. Mama's sister call all the way from England." She pronounced it Eng-er-land.

Curious though I was to know how she was aware I had a message at all, I simply smiled and thanked her, and drove on. As I reached Gwen's cottage, her own maid dashed out into the road, and with equal enthusiasm, called me in to receive my message. These two seemed to be taking a rather more than expected interest in my affairs, so naturally, my curiosity was further piqued.

All was then revealed. I mentioned to Gwen that I'd now had two advance warnings of my message. Not that I objected, I explained, but the attention it had received seemed rather disproportionately intense, so I couldn't help but wonder what would happen when I really had some news. Would there be throngs of maids lining the road waving me through? Would there be banners and balloons? Justifiably disregarding my flippant remarks, Gwen explained why the two girls were so excited.

Our telephone system was a kind of magic to our Zulu helpers. They were fascinated by it, and whenever they heard the phone ring and there was no one to see them, they rushed to pick it up, listening to these speaking machines with delight. Consequently, they knew everything that was going on in the valley, and took a childlike glee in passing on the news to their counterparts on the neighbouring farms and homesteads. After all, they could make local calls themselves at no cost and it was usually the housemaid who answered the calls in the first place. The very fact that my sister had phoned from somewhere that could have been another planet to them was reason enough to give me star appeal.

There was no harm in it, and certainly no malice intended in the circulation of our news, but privacy had no place in their lives, so they failed to understand where it fitted into ours. For a time, I wrestled with the conflicting feelings of annoyance at such an intrusion into my personal life and amusement at the speed at which information travelled in this unsophisticated and technologically primitive society. Eventually, though, I succumbed to the prevailing attitude of 'if you can't beat them....', and took to asking Bongi for my news and messages. She certainly had a more reliable and accurate memory for the details than both the Ellenses combined.

Trading Store Treats

Elandskop village itself didn't really amount to much, even after further investigation. There was, however, a single shop of rather surprisingly substantial proportions. Dawood Asmal's General Dealers was not only an absolute treasure trove but also a complete culture shock

Imagine coming from a country where shops are almost uniformly clinical in their layout, and where every food item on offer was cling-wrapped to the virtual extinction of the consumable it was designed to protect. Then picture a first encounter with a real honest-to-goodness African-style trading store which sells everything from welly boots to frozen chicken feet; a store whose only real concession to hygiene involved hanging sticky fly-catcher strips around, on which the poor victims are still wriggling vainly even as we buy our supplies of meat and marge.

It follows then that the first time I went to Asmal's I was somewhat unprepared for the rather basic quality of the store; I was shocked by the apparent lack of order or attention to cleanliness. In contrast, I was totally fascinated by the wealth and variety of the goods it sold.

The shop was located in a dip below the road, to the side and a bit behind the garage. You had to go down a sloping driveway to reach the low, wide-fronted building which sported the name Dawood Asmal's General Dealers rather grandly in large red letters on its shabby white-washed fascia.

In front of the store, goods were piled up in haphazard profusion: sacks of the best Impala maize meal; buckets of various shapes and sizes; five litre cans of paraffin for the ubiquitous oil lamps, and all manner of other bulky goods, including sacks of charcoal, wood and large black cooking pots on legs that looked like witches' cauldrons, but are called *potjes* (pronounced poykies).

There were always a few pickannins loitering around outside the shop too. This was the Zulu word for youngsters of indeterminate age, and they were the unofficial 'help'. At a guess, they were probably around eleven or twelve years old, and should probably have been at school. However, the school of life was obviously more attractive and certainly more lucrative, as for a few cents or some sweets, they helped carry bags to cars and sacks of meal to trucks, often struggling under their burdens; it should also be said that they mostly looked distinctly under nourished.

Inside, the store stretched back some distance and, despite the gloom, gave the impression of space and size, while being crammed to the ceiling with stock. Here, you could buy clothes and shoes, blankets and tin baths, candles and lamps. You could also buy tools for almost any purpose, including pangas (a kind of machete), knives, gardening tools, crow bars and sledge hammers.

In another part of the store were bolts of fabric and sewing materials, together with one or two traditional hand operated sewing machines; then there were the fridges full of the dubious delicacies the Zulu people favour such as chicken livers, necks and feet, not to mention parts of other animals that didn't even bear description.

I tried not to be revolted by the sight of these gruesome reminders of our carnivorous customs; after all, the French eat frogs' legs, truffles and snails. Nevertheless, I found it difficult to believe people could actually enjoy munching on a gristle-packed, sharply clawed foot that looked as if it had only recently been treading earth on the end of a moving limb.

There was a slight but all pervading smell of rotting meat, mixed with the earthy aromas of hot dust and unwashed bodies which always seemed to hang on the air. To be fair, this was not unique to Asmal's, but seemed to be an identifying odour in every trading store. I expect they were subject to unreliable electricity supplies either from the main grid or from dicey generators, and things simply went 'off' in the heat.

In the centre of the store, piled high to make a kind of island, were the bulk sized sacks of rice, sugar and maize meal placed together with boxes of vegetables, most of which had seen a week or two since they had been plucked, picked or dug up, but were still sold as 'fresh' produce. At the counter, Asmal's sold bread in half or whole loaves, milk and almost unnaturally yellow cheese. Cigarettes could be bought here either in packets of twenty or thirty, but also singly for those end-of-the-month days; that being said, these were not as popular as Boxer, the favourite hand rolling tobacco, which was coarse, dark and so strong that it stripped the back of your throat with one puff. Papers for making cigarettes were available too, but I mostly saw roll-ups made with newspaper or even hard toilet paper – why waste precious 'baccy' money on expensive slivers of tissue you were only going to burn?

There were also a number of patent medicines and toiletries available behind the counter, and on the counter itself, various sweets, gums and other delectables including a large jar of Chappies, which were a cheap kind of flavoured chewing gum. My daughters developed quite a strong Chappie habit, stimulated by the four 'Did you know' general knowledge questions printed on the inside of each wrapper, and I must say, they used to come up with the most bizarre titbits of useless information. For instance, I recall Jojo telling me earnestly once that the Romans used to use urine in their toothpaste. I'm not sure which surprised me more: the fact itself as presented by a pre-schooler or that the Romans actually used toothpaste at all.

Unfortunately, it sometimes didn't work as planned. Obviously the wrappers were machine cut, so on occasions they would get one that only had the first part of the information. Very frustrating for the children, but great for prompting them to look further than a sweet paper for their knowledge. The next move up to books was not such a huge step for them, so I suppose you could say they had something to be grateful to Chappies for. I'm not sure how many educators and health experts would agree with me though, and can imagine only too well their disapproval of candy induced learning.

Chappies were also used as currency by many shopkeepers and not being one to miss a trick, our Dawood adopted the scheme too. If I bought goods at Asmal's to the value of say R9,98 and I paid with a R10 note, he gave me the change in Chappies for the children. This must have saved him a fortune and probably paid for the family pile, which I'm sure he probably had in an affluent Asian area of Pietermaritzburg. Indeed, there must have been many a trading store proprietor that owed his healthy bank balance to 'Chappie change'.

My absolute favourite section of the shop was the cosmetics and toiletries shelf; not because I was a dedicated user of make-up, but because I could find things there which I'd never seen in my life before: There were all sorts of strange concoctions and many types of 'pillies'. There were Grandpa powders, which are a form of pain killer and flu treatment that have to be taken in water. You could also buy snuff in little yellow tins, which I thought was something that had gone out of fashion in the last century. Nonetheless, it seemed to be extremely popular, especially with women, and I often saw them taking pinches of it.

However, my number one in the bizarre cosmetics chart was the product with the rather tongue-in-cheek name of 'He-man'. It came in a bottle enclosed in a cardboard box displaying an image of a naked man with outstretched arms, rather similar to Leonardo da Vinci's Vitruvian man. When I first saw it advertised, I thought it had something to do with muscle building, and imagined some kind of Chinese herbal preparation, so when Bongi asked me to get some for her from Asmal's, I raised a mental eyebrow, but said nothing; perhaps, I mused, she wanted to turn some of her extra padding to good use.

Surprisingly, Mr Asmal was not so reticent, although he was normally rather formal with the farmers and their families. Small and very dark skinned, he tended to wear loose white shirts over dark trousers, so that when he came to greet me from the gloom of the shop, it looked as if a disembodied shirt was floating towards me. Then he smiled and the shirt was joined by some grinning teeth. By the time he reached me, I was so absorbed in the surrealism of the moment that nothing would have surprised me.

After the usual courtesies, he asked me what he could get for me. I went through my list and when I came to the He-man, his eyes widened in astonishment:

"My word, madam, what will you be needing that for? May I say you are quite light enough already."

Thinking he was referring to my weight, I shook my head.

"No, no, it's not for me. I'm not trying to build up muscles, Mr Asmal. It's for Bongile, Mrs Ellens's maid. I think she's trying to get stronger."

With that, he broke into a long peal of laughter.

"Oh no, madam, He-man is not for making muscles. It's for making the skin go pale. See here," he pointed to the small print on the box, "It's a skin lightener. That's why I was surprised that you asked for it. You are already so much paler than most of us, madam. A lot of the girls here use it, although I can understand that for you it is a strange name."

When I handed the He-man over to Bongi, I asked her why she wanted to make her skin lighter. I pointed out that her natural colour was not very dark, and it suited her well. She looked down and chuckled, her whole body shaking gently.

"I don't know, missy Val. Maybe I ask you the same. Why you want to make your skin darker?"

She had a point, I thought, thinking of the pleasure I felt in my increasingly tanned appearance. Fashions are never based on reason, are they? It seemed this reality held true even in the backwaters of rural Africa.

CHAPTER 6

Close Encounters Of The Social Kind

To *braai* or not to *braai*

Anyone who has spent some time in South Africa will know that the principal form of entertainment is the *Braai* or as the rest of the world knows it, the Barbecue.

The *braai* is the core of almost every social gathering that takes place in the South African home. There does not need to be any excuse or reason to have a *braai*; it can be a spontaneous affair that can take place at any time of day or night – even breakfast. It can also take place anywhere: in the garden, on the patio, on a balcony, in a car park behind the car, on the beach, or in the bush. In fact, at the most basic level, as long as there is meat, firewood, a piece of wire mesh to use as a grill and some matches or a lighter, it's possible to make a *braai*.

Braais can be quite formal as well. My first was at a friend's house in Durban. The host and hostess lived in an elegant hacienda style villa with a tiled entertainment area in which there was a built-in *braai plek*. It seemed to come complete with gas burners to replace the rather messier charcoal that was customary - perhaps a rather clinical concession to up-market living, because it lacked something of the atmosphere of good smoky coals.

As this was an anniversary party, all the food and drink were supplied, although most guests took along a bottle of wine or six pack of beer to show willing. One thing I did notice, though, was that there seemed to be a form of gender segregation in evidence. All the men stood around the sizzling sausages holding beer bottles and intermittently giving the grilling meat furtive prods with whatever they were holding in their other hands: forks, penknives, fire tools and even sticks of wood could be seen darting in and out, almost as if they couldn't resist the impulse to take control. The women, meanwhile, were grouped at a distance from the grill and were conducting their own party, drinking wine from proper glasses and paying no attention to the food or the men.

I was somewhat surprised by this, especially when I was drawn inexorably into the female group, so I asked my new acquaintances if this was normal practice at a party. Almost all of them laughed self-consciously and admitted that *braais* certainly were always like this, and no, they didn't know why, it was just that way. Of course, plenty of hypotheses were put forward: it gave the women a break from cooking; the men only ever talked about sport which was boring; it was the only chance the women had to get together and talk about their own interests. No one really seemed to know for sure, and I doubt if they had ever really thought about it. It was clearly something of a 'sacred cow' that was simply accepted and no longer needed discussion. Being a compulsive observer of life's more curious quirks, however, I decided it not only needed more discussion, it most definitely needed further investigation.

The next *braai* we were invited to was on a neighbouring farm shortly after our installation in the cottage. Our hosts, Rob and his wife, Sandy, were a relaxed, cheerful couple who had emigrated from the big city to try their hand at market gardening in the valley. This event became much more my standard for what a good *braai* should be. Firstly, in their back garden, which separated the house from the farm land, there was a proper charcoal fire built on a metal sheet supported by bricks to raise it to waist height. The fire itself was surrounded by stones to contain it. On top of the stones a large square grid had been balanced and it was on this that the meat was grilled.

Everyone invited brought cooler bags full of beer and wine, and the wives all brought some form of eats. Mostly this was a salad of some description, but there were also foil-wrapped garlic breads, rolls, sweets and a selection of scrumptious looking desserts. I was particularly fond of making and eating pasta salad, so as usual I took along a large bowl of macaroni à la Val. It was liberally doused with mayonnaise and filled with an assortment of tomato, chopped egg, diced ham, garlic and a variety of herbs, in particular oregano, which grew prolifically in Willem Ellens's garden.

A trestle table had been set up under the spreading branches of a Golden Oak tree and covered with paper cloths. All contributions to the food were gratefully received and put on the table until it was creaking threateningly with the variety and number of dishes. At one end of the trestle were two 5 litre boxes of Chateau Carton (our own name for the local plonk), one white and one red, and beside the table was a tin bath full of ice cubes in which full beer bottles were embedded as quickly as others were removed and emptied.

Rob and Sandy also grew *naartjies*, or mandarins as Europeans know them, on their acres so there was a lovely arrangement of them piled into a pyramid at the centre of the table. I pondered this precarious pile and wondered if anyone would have the courage to disturb it and risk a total and embarrassing collapse.

Once we were all armed with drinks, I noticed 'it' happening again: the gradual, insidious and surreptitious separation of the sexes until two distinct groups were formed. Within half an hour of everyone's arrival, there, gathered round the *braai*, were all the men discussing either the fire, or the rugby and cricket scores, while the women found chairs and formed a semi circle under the trees. Some of the mums had even brought their knitting and embroidery, and chatted away cheerfully while their hands were productively occupied in churning out the winter woollies for the kids or tray cloths for granny. The pattern was being repeated: different people, different surroundings and a totally different social circle, but the same behaviour again.

This time I broke ranks and, moving into the sacred circle round the fire, I decided to ask for a masculine opinion on the reason for the segregation. Bill, with unusual tact, refrained from comment, but the other men regarded each other bashfully and came up with nothing more convincing than the odd inane remark along the lines of 'a woman's place' and 'a man's job' and so on. Again, no clues. I withdrew fairly promptly feeling very much like the Druid among a bunch of Christian crusaders; not to mention being a clearly inhibiting presence in the discussion of the ideal rugby tackle and what "that idiot Pienaar" or "Van the Man" should have done when he "had the ball". I was also thoroughly baffled. In the UK we'd been a lot more integrated in our social habits.

These first two experiences of a *braai* were both lunchtime affairs that went on until about six in the evening. During the afternoon, a large quantity of beer, wine and food was consumed, despite which no one appeared to be the worse for wear. But then, this was normal. I came to expect it as a familiar routine when invited to lunch by neighbours and friends. I also came to expect, and eventually accept, the natural division between the sexes that occurred at all these gatherings. I still didn't really understand why, though.

Some light did eventually glimmer faintly on a possible reason much later on in our social education. On this occasion we were on a weekend hiking trip with another family on the banks of the Umkhomazi river. Kowie and Sue and their two small sons were those rare creatures in Natal, Afrikaners, and Kowie (pronounced Kuvvy) was certain he was the only one among us who knew how to make a decent fire. It was in his genes, he claimed. This conviction was inevitably going to bring him into conflict with Bill, who had gone totally native by this time and was also unshakeably sure he was the best fire builder in the southern hemisphere.

The Umkhomazi runs through steep sided valleys of bush covered hills. In places, it runs deep and wide in the summer, but in our mountain foothills, it was narrower, steeper and shallower, tossing and winding itself over a rocky bed of broad slabs of stone. The spot where we had chosen to spend our afternoon offered a stony beach with large, still pools where the fish were easily visible. There were also bushy trees for shade; all the children could play safely in the shallow waters, and it was an ideal retreat for a lazy, relaxed lunch. Or so it seemed.

The two men had been fishing and had proudly caught enough for us to have a fish *braai*. The first stirrings of primeval combat began when I asked innocently who was going to be in charge of the fire. The "I'll do it" came in unison, as did the subsequent glaring match which was intended by each to intimidate the other into submission. Hoping to avert an escalation of hostilities, Sue and I suggested they both did it. With grudging accord, and without further communication, the two prepared a ring of rocks as the basis for the fire while the children were commissioned to find as many dry sticks as possible for igniting the lumps of charcoal. Thus the *braai plek* was prepared without a shot being fired.

However, the truce was not to last long. They couldn't resist squaring up to each other again. When Kowie went off to find more wood, Bill immediately huddled over the fire to re-arrange it to his own liking. On his return, Kowie noted in a voice loaded with suppressed rage that 'someone' had been messing with the embers and grimly set to work to 'right' them. Bill spluttered his indignation and they embarked on a barely audible row that was conducted through clenched teeth and closed lips. Even a ventriloquist would have been impressed. Again, we wives intervened and peace was tenuously restored. Both were forbidden, on pain of beer starvation, to touch the fire until it was ready for the cooking.

It was an uneasy lull, though, and the tension was only dissipated when the fish were sizzling on the grill in their foil wrappings. The aroma was tantalising and combined with *mealie* cobs baked at the edge of the coals, we were looking forward to a heavenly *braai* with a difference.

I thought that would be the end of the issue, but after the last morsels had been wiped off the picnic plates, Sue blithely suggested that we have some coffee. We'd brought a flask along with us, but it had gone tepid after the first cups had been poured and would have to be re-heated. The fires needed stirring, both literally and figuratively.

Once again, battle ensued as to who should take charge, but by this time, the feminine factor had seen enough, and we shooed both men away to the river and banished them for the remainder of the day. Oddly enough, once the object of their dispute was removed from their field of play, they went off happily and were soon heard laughing and joking in their normal state of camaraderie.

Sue and I discussed this phenomenon at some length, and decided that the South African male's obsession with tending the flames was inherited at the latest from the *voortrekkers* where the ultimate responsibility for feeding his family came down to the *boer's* ability not just to find food, but to keep the fire going. At the earliest, though, it could be a more general instinct going back to much more ancient times, and manifested so noticeably in South Africa simply because the *braai* was such a standard means of entertaining and cooking. It also gave one possible explanation for the social separation at larger gatherings: men are biologically and anthropologically attracted to the cooking fire like magnets and have an irresistible urge to tend it. Women, on the other hand, have no such burning instincts.

From a spit to a storm

One New Year's Eve at the farm, we decided to hold a big party to celebrate the fact of Bill's new and financially rewarding job in Durban. We'd been through a rough patch when he was out of work for some months, and the Ellenses had been unreservedly supportive and generous, so we wanted to put on a good show in thanks for their unfailing kindness.

It had taken a year or two to adjust to having Christmas and New Year in the middle of summer, but now we revelled in it and dispensed happily with Christmas trees and turkey in favour of *braais* in the garden or even on the beach. This year, we intended to go one step further and roast a lamb on a spit.

We invited all our friends from the neighbouring holdings, and Bill asked a number of both new and former colleagues and their partners. This was interesting in itself because many of these city dwellers had no idea about how to dress for a weekend party on a rural farm. I watched with interest as the yuppie element arrived with their smart cars, smart clothes and smarter girlfriends. The highly groomed, elegant damsels stepped out onto the dense, springy kikuyu grass in their spiked high-heeled shoes, promptly sank several centimetres, and got stuck. This didn't do much for their attempts at unruffled poise, but, I thought irreverently, at least the worms would appreciate the extra oxygen.

Then, I smiled benignly at the young lady who asked me where she could plug her hairdryer in, savouring the moment briefly before apologising that we had no electricity. Her face dropped in dismay. The best part, though, was assuring another crease-free beauty that of course she could iron her blouse, as I proceeded to hand her the heavy old flat irons that had to be heated up on the stove before use. She gave me an only barely concealed shot of venom before politely declining my offer.

We had enlisted the whole Kheswa clan to help us clear out the big barn next to the milking shed. It was solid but a bit dilapidated through lack of recent use. There were several old farm machines that had to be pushed, heaved or pulled out of the way, and the whole area had to be swept clean and decorated with as many balloons and streamers as we could collect together. Kheswa himself helped with cheerful gusto, encouraged by the promise of the food and drink to be supplied later on, as indeed everyone on the farm was invited. It was evident that he was for once prepared to put his normal back problems on hold for a job that would be rewarded by such potentially mouth-watering fare.

We piled straw bales around the sides of the barn for seating and erected trestles made from old doors on which to heap the food. The drink was confined to the inevitable beer and boxes of wine. One of the wonderful aspects of living in a grape growing country is that you can always buy good table wine at absurdly low prices for very generous quantities. In all the years I lived in South Africa, I don't ever recall drinking a bad one, even our staple, the cheap Chateau Carton.

We even cranked up the old generator so that we could have some music. In the event, though, it was so noisy that it drowned out all but the hardest rock played at full volume. The Rolling Stones were no match for the great Lister 'genny'.

About four hours before the party was due to begin, Bill, together with Kheswa, Jacob and David, started setting up the spit. This went reasonably well until they tried to attach the lamb itself. The problem was that they had to tie its legs together over the top of the spit pole, but given the fact that it hadn't long come out of the cold of the fridge, it still had the stiffness of rigors in its bones. Every time Kheswa or Bill managed to force a pair of legs together, one of them would slip out of grasp and spring back to stick rigidly and obstinately out of reach. It was slimy with marinade and grease, so hands slid every which way and the decidedly deceased lamb seemed to take on a new life of its own. The fits of helpless laughter that this evoked the first few times soon went sour, and expressions slowly transformed from hilarious to stonily determined. They circled the carcass, scratched chins and heads and gesticulated emphatically, but the stubborn beast would not comply.

About half an hour later and in a fit of frustrated genius, Kheswa evolved a method for tying each leg individually to its opposite pole on the frame using a length of string. Then together he and Bill pulled the string from each side so that when the legs met in the middle, David could quickly tie them together. So simple, yet so effective. Within minutes, the three of them were grinning happily through their grease smeared faces.

Finally, the fire was lit, and Kheswa was awarded the job of chief spit turner, a task he embraced with vigour, along with plenty of beer. This was the top job as far as he was concerned and his smile was a vision of white teeth from ear to ear.

Up till now, none of us had paid much attention to the weather. The afternoon had been sunny and hot, and while it was usual for us to have a quick in and out thunder storm around four o'clock, we hadn't had one that day. The first thought we gave it was when, as dusk was descending, we heard the threatening rumbles of thunder.

The spit was doing nicely, and the new year's revellers were all gathered round giving comments of encouragement to a beaming Kheswa. He was in his element. I began to think he'd missed his vocation, as he was proving to be a slick entertainer. However, looking up at the darkening skies, I realised the gloom wasn't only due to the oncoming night.

100

Smelling at last the rain in the air, I ran up to the cottage and unearthed an old tarpaulin from the back veranda, which I then dragged back down to the circle round the spit. Ear marking the four tallest men in the group, I persuaded them to be the tent poles for supporting the outspread tarpaulin in the event that the storm hit us as I suspected it would quite shortly. It did.

With one almighty crack, and a bolt of lightning that split the sky straight down the middle, the wind rushed in, followed shortly by torrential rain. Most of our party guests made for the cover of the barn and carried on where they left off. The laughing and drinking continued unabated to the sound of the rain hurling itself onto the tin roof. It drowned any possibility for conversation as well as the noise from both the generator and the music.

The four spit protectors doggedly held the cover over a chuckling Kheswa as they mournfully eyed the bright entrance of the barn through the curtain of rain that was streaming off the edge of their shelter. I stifled a moment's guilt. As long as I kept them well supplied with beer, I felt sure they would survive.

Luckily the storm didn't last too long, and within an hour had eased off to a soft drizzle. Unfortunately, this didn't let up so we were forced to stay inside anyway.

As soon as the lamb was deemed to be sufficiently done, we hauled the whole contraption into the barn where Bill, as ceremoniously as his somewhat inebriated state allowed, began to carve thick, juicy slices of meat for a queue of hungry guests. I breathed a sigh of relief as he reached the last one. Then, brandishing his knife with uncharacteristic bravado, he lurched off out into the rain. It was rather a grand, if wobbly, exit. His feet seemed to be in conflict as to which way to take him, but I guessed he was just going out to relieve himself and didn't want to have to say so.

A couple of minutes later, Bill was back again, moisture dripping from the end of this hair, but now he looked miraculously sober. It was a momentary illusion, though. Almost creeping up to me, he whispered something in my ear, then burped, then apologised. Looking at his deathly white face, I had the idea that something had scared him, and quite badly too. After pulling him gently back through the door away from the noise, I asked him what was wrong. He leant back against the wall, sucked some air through his teeth and then with supreme effort, he exhaled one word, "leopard!"

"What on earth do you mean? What leopard?" I asked incredulously.

"Was having a pee," his voice slurred at me. "Over there. The fence." He flapped a hand in the direction of the nearest paddock. "The ground got up an' ran away. Was 'orrible. Sure it was that leopard you said was here. Sure of it. Ran low. S'belly on the ground. Don't tell anyone, right? Don't want to scare 'em." And he slid smoothly to the ground and went to sleep. It definitely was sleep, because he was snoring loudly within seconds.

Slipping back into the barn, I managed to find Kheswa who was still presiding over his lamb and carving off chunks for anyone whose stomach could still find a gap for more. I rather think he was helping to close a few of his own gaps too, because he seemed very reluctant to leave his post. Nevertheless, I persuaded him to come and help me carry Bill up to the house, and while we were manhandling his wayward, uncooperative body slowly up the path, I told Kheswa about the 'leopard'.

The old man looked at me thoughtfully then smiled his gap-toothed smile.

"Mister Bill see no leopard, mama. Leopard no like people. Only one here and she stay up there," he jerked his head to the mountaintop where I knew I had seen one before. "What Mister Bill see is *leguan* (Iguana). He not scared for people. He not scared for anything and I many times see *leguan* here on farm. He no hurt anyone."

The next morning I was carrying a tray of coffee and rolls out into the garden for our overnight guests when I heard Bill elaborating on his leopard story to the clear amazement of his entire audience. I was surprised that he even remembered it.

"There I was," he exclaimed, laughing at the image already in his mind, "just doing a spot of midnight watering, when what do you think I'm giving a wetting to but a friggin' leopard!" The audience was laughing at the image now too.

Bill went on to the punch line, "Must've thought I was trying to change his spots for him. Couldn't have that now, could he?" More uproarious laughter followed exclamations of admiration for his bravery.

I thought about what Kheswa had told me. An iguana didn't sound nearly so impressive. Or even so interesting. I decided to keep quiet. It had been a great party, and Bill was having his moment in the sun. He was clearly still convinced that he'd seen the leopard and he was embellishing the tale brilliantly. I regarded the scene indulgently. Why spoil a good story with the less than glamorous truth?

CHAPTER 7

Learning Curves

Classroom clangers

For the first year on the farm, and even beyond that, Jodie stayed at home with Mo and was quite happy playing with Bongi and any of the other Kheswa children who turned up, but mostly with David. He was tirelessly patient and kind to these two small things, and taught first Jo to ride the farm ponies and then later Mo, when she was big enough to sit in front of him and stay upright on her own. Walking time and time again round the broad sweep of the garden, coaching, encouraging and holding them when they threatened to slide off, David demonstrated all the gifts of a born trainer. He spoke to Jojo in Zulu and, as children do, she picked up the words and quickly learnt to speak to him in his own language – granted, it was a pidgin variety of Zulu, but she was no more articulate in English at that time either.

They also had friends in the valley where there were other young families with small children, and they often spent whole days away, only to come home at night, dirty, sunburnt and happy. So the days, months and then the years passed. Their games were of their own invention, as we had no external stimuli in the form of TV, and had brought no toys with us from England, so they were forced to rely on their greatest resource: their imagination. It was a precious time and I loved watching the mini dramas, and even mini series they enacted as well as the model houses and farms they built from stones, grass and sticks. They rolled naked in sand and mud alike, whether at Bongi's kraal or on the farm itself, and when they got too plastered with muck, I rinsed them off under the tap outside the flat, which was really intended for watering the garden.

Nevertheless, by the beginning of our second year, Jodie was three and a half and started pleading to go to the local farm school in Elandskop. Her friends in the valley were already going and loved it. The little school was run by Gwen's daughter, 'Auntie Moreen', so naturally Jo was keen to go. Any connection to 'Gork' was going to be appealing.

Like all young mums, I was reluctant to take that huge step of losing my firstborn to the education system, so I resisted the pleas for some time and she was nearly four before she finally got her way and I delivered her to the school for her first day.

Then, as well as now, formal school didn't begin in South Africa until a child was six years old, so from the age of three to six, many children went to play school. During the last year of this stage, they usually received preparation for 'big' school in the form of learning the alphabet and some basic reading and counting. So there was quite a structure to our farm school, despite the lack of lessons as such. They didn't just play. They painted and did craft work; they had story time and rest time; all in readiness for the day when learning and homework would take on a more serious complexion.

'Big' school was a major step for the farm children because most of them became weekly boarders in Richmond. They went to school on Monday morning and came home again on Friday. They also had to wear a uniform, which was another change from play school, so the transition from Aunty Moreen's to Richmond Primary was a life-changing landmark in these farm children's lives. The formative years at the little school in Elandskop were even more precious as a result.

The school building itself was a friendly, inviting place built of red brick. It was set on a slight rise and the play ground appeared to be on a man-made mound with its brightly painted slide, swing and see-saw grouped around the top. Like many remote village schools, it was very small and only catered for the local children. This allowed for an intimacy and personal approach that would have been impossible in a city environment.

On the days she attended, Jodie couldn't wait to get there. In her hurry to scramble out of the car, she mostly gave me a sort of sideswipe peck somewhere near my cheek and waved a rather cursory good bye before scampering off to the gently embracing setting that Moreen had created. And, as time went on, my little Mo became increasingly aware of what she was missing and distinctly disgruntled about being left at home.

One day when I was collecting Jojo from her morning at school, I noticed a faint chill surrounding Moreen's greeting and farewell. Puzzled by so marked a change in her normal warm reception, I asked Jojo how school had gone that morning. The bubbling enthusiasm revealed nothing out of the ordinary. I was a little unsettled though. Trying to cut through the artless prattle to see if anything had transpired to cause the breath of frost I'd noticed, I prodded Jojo into telling me what they had been doing in more detail than usual. Story telling. Aah. So what story did Jojo tell? I encouraged her lightly, keeping my eyes on the rock-strewn road ahead.

She started to giggle in remembrance. "I told her how horrid you are, Mummy. I told her that when I'm naughty you lock me in the cupboard. But I didn't mean it. It was just a story." My heart sank. Did Jo tell Aunty Moreen it was just a story? More giggles. No, she didn't. My heart didn't re-surface. Ah well. There wasn't much I could do without appearing to 'protest too much'. I could feel my reputation crumbling around my ears.

However, children do invent things all the time, and so the next time I collected Jo from school, I suggested that she apologise to her teacher for telling tales. Clutching my hand, and grinning disarmingly, Jodie confessed that her story wasn't true, and as if to add authenticity, said that we didn't even have a cupboard big enough to hold her. I cringed. That wasn't true either. To my relief, Moreen told me to think no more of it as she knew full well she shouldn't believe everything her charges told her. "You'd be amazed by some of the things I hear," she soothed diplomatically, but I was still left with the feeling that she wasn't entirely convinced. I couldn't blame her.

My child could be very persuasive and had a very fertile imagination. I was sometimes scandalised by the things she told people with such wide-eyed innocence. Normally, it was her sister who was the villain of the piece, and it was just my bad luck that on this occasion, with this rather important figure, it was my turn to assume that role.

With a notion that Jojo had somehow unwittingly blotted my copybook, I pleaded with her to stick to either the truth or complete fantasy involving fictional people when regaling her class with the fruits of her invention. She promised and was appealingly sorry for the gaff. She also promptly forgot the incident, and carried on as before.

Balance was nonetheless restored, and our lives continued as usual. Mo, however, became ever more plaintive on the days when Jojo went off to school. She sulked, cried and generally developed into a miniature tyrant whenever her sister wasn't there. Unfortunately for me, Jojo backed her up and begged me to let Mo go with her. I knew the rules though. No child was allowed to attend the play school until they were three. It was simply not possible. I explained to both of them as plainly as I could that a not-quite-two-and-a-half year old couldn't pass for three, however much of a wonder child we might think she was, and she was certainly too big to hide in Jodie's schoolbag – a proposition put to me in all earnest by my eldest.

Regrettably, this didn't stop the pleading, and after weeks of whining and tears from Mo, together with Jojo's persistent pestering, I was beginning to develop 'nerves'. Every time I heard one or other of them say "Maaaaaamie" in that typically wheedling tone of voice, I tensed up instantly, and only relaxed when I was sure they weren't pulling out the same old horse to flog again.

Eventually, however, it came up once too often, and I snapped. Following one particularly irritating case of the 'maaamies,' I retaliated with a harsh "I know it's a pain, but Mo's too young and that's all there is to it. It's what Aunty Moreen told me, so that's the end of it." I suppose I vainly hoped that if I quoted her teacher, whom she adored, Jojo would accept it as truth. Naïve maybe, but in my experience small children usually idolise their teachers and are much more inclined to believe them than their own parents. "Miss" or "Sir" is the next in line to God in their eyes.

I lived to rue this particular outburst. The following afternoon, Jojo's friends from the valley came to play, and one of the first things her little buddy took delight in telling me was that Aunty Moreen was cross with both me and my daughter. This was news indeed. I hadn't seen her when I did the fetching from school as she was talking to another parent, so had no forewarning of the gloom that was about to descend.

Jojo never liked reporting bad news herself and even in later years, would rather hide the evidence than let me know there was anything wrong. I took her to one side and pressed her to tell me what had happened and why Aunty Moreen was cross.

Apparently, Jodie had decided to challenge the entire school system. She had taken the bold step of taking her campaign to lower the school starting age to the one person she now saw as being responsible for causing her sister's distress.

"I just told her what you said, Mummy. I said it was her fault Mo couldn't come to school and that you said she was a pain, and...," she ran out of words, guilt suddenly overwhelming her for having done something to upset her Aunty Moreen. Not, it appeared, for having dropped her poor mother in the mire.

There was no pleading my way out of this one. My copybook was now severely stained, not just blotted. The trouble was that, but for one small, apparently insignificant word – 'you' in place of 'it', I might have been able to explain what I'd really said. To say, "you're a pain" is so direct though, so rude and so much not what I had actually blurted out. This time my heart didn't only sink, it remained firmly wallowing in the depths.

Suffering from a surfeit of over reaction, it seemed then that there was only one thing to do. It was the end of the school term, the holidays were upon us and under the weight of reflected guilt and shame, I decided I couldn't send Jojo back to the farm school. I had found a job in Richmond, so instead I enrolled her in another nursery school close to my work. Incidentally, this was also lovely and what was even better, they were prepared to take Mo too because they were licensed as a crèche as well. However, to this day I wonder if my daughter's uncanny ability to place not just one, but both feet firmly in her mouth hadn't made me overly sensitive. Perhaps I shouldn't have considered Jojo's little friend a reliable witness. Maybe Moreen had not been cross with me at all. Given her patience, experience and wisdom with young children, it would certainly have been out of character. I just never took the risk of finding out.

Although my daughters didn't start learning Zulu at school until later in their education, the interaction we had with the Kheswa family ensured that we all absorbed at least some of their beautiful, lyrical language. Indeed, tucked away as we were in rural Kwazulu Natal, we had more exposure to Zulu than we had to the other official language of the time, Afrikaans.

For Europeans with no previous knowledge or background, Zulu is a language for the vocal contortionist. Peppered with clicks and pops formed in totally inaccessible parts of the mouth, it seems almost impossible to pronounce. To master it completely, I'm sure lessons should preferably begin in the cradle, but definitely at a very early age.

We were very keen to learn at least a smattering, so that we could open lines of communication with our host province. Initially, we picked up the rather romantic formal greetings from Bongi, who enjoyed teaching us as much as our tongues could cope with. We learnt how to say hello, or good morning, which is *sawubona* when speaking to one person, but *sanibonani* for more than one.

We learnt the farewells too: *sala kahle*, pronounced *'gashlé'* is addressed to the one who stays behind and I was told it actually means 'stay in peace'; *hamba kahle* is said to the one leaving and means 'go in peace'. To be polite, of course, you have to ask after someone's welfare after greeting them, and for this there is *unjani* meaning 'how are you?' to which the answer might be *ngikhona*, I'm fine, with the 'h' after the 'k' so soft as to be almost silent.

An entire greeting is a lovely poetic refrain, as the music of the language, with its stress on the ends of the words, makes it sound like a litany. A typical exchange between two people could go like this:

Person A: *Sawubona* - Good morning/hello

Person B: *Sawubona* - Good morning

Person A: *Unjani*? - How are you?

Person B: *Wenjani*? - And how are you?

Person A: *Ngikhona* - I'm fine thanks

Person B: *Namingikhona* - I'm fine too

Person A: *Sala kahle* - Goodbye/stay in peace

Person B: *Hamba kahle* - Goodbye/go in peace

Wenjani is in fact *wena unjani* but when spoken, it runs into one word.

Then there were the normal courtesy words: 'please' in our area was *siza*, although there were other variations. At the time I thought the word for thank you was simply *yabonga*, but I have since discovered that this is a commonly made slip as, according to my dictionary, the complete word is *ngiyabonga* to which you add *kakhulu* if you want to say 'thanks very much'.

Sometimes I was addressed formally, and the polite *unkosikazi* would then be used, being the Zulu word for 'madam', although I was more often greeted with the shorter *unkosana*, which may have been a local corruption of the correct version. It was mostly used if I didn't know the person and so more formality was required on both sides. Likewise, the polite address for a man is *umnumzane*, but Bill was very flattered and also a little humbled when his staff at worked addressed him as *nkosi*, which is rather more of an honour as it means 'chief' or even 'king'. On the other hand, they also teased him by calling him 'old one' or *omdala*, especially on those occasions when they decided he was being too bossy.

Our collection of words slowly built up and before long I also knew that a young lady was an *intombi* and a boy was an *umfana*, while a mother was simply *umama* which probably explains why they were so comfortable addressing me as 'mama'. With my two small daughters mostly in tow, it must have seemed the obvious English name to give me.

I found the local people to be naturally courteous, very friendly and always ready for laughter, although I am forced to admit in hindsight that some of the courtesy was probably due to the social conditioning wrought by the system. Nevertheless, they had an inbuilt graciousness that was manifested in the almost regal quality of their language.

112

There was another side to their vocabulary, however, that amused me no end. Several words for some of the more modern every day items were almost completely onomatopoeic or adaptations of our own terms. I gathered examples of these with relish.

An *isithuthu*, for instance, is a motorbike. Remembering not to make much of the 'h', and pronouncing it more like '*i-stutu*', you can almost hear the puttering sound of a small 50 cc. On the other hand, the word for an ordinary bicycle becomes an *ibhayisikeli*, which is not far removed from our own word. Then there was my personal favourite, *igunda gunda*, which doesn't appear in my dictionary but was Kheswa's term for a tractor; think of the sound of an old diesel engine and you're right there with it.

Others that tickled me were a radio, which is an i-*rediyo*, while a kettle is an *igedlela* and paraffin, a daily necessity in rural parts, is *uphalafini* – again, a silent 'h'. These were simple, but charming local solutions to latter day inventions, and I loved them. In point of fact, the Zulus do what so many other languages have done when new developments require new words. Think, for example, of the verb 'to iron' as in ironing clothes. This is *ayina*. They simply adopt the existing international or English terms and 'Zulufy' them.

There were, of course, some phrases we would have preferred not to learn quite so early on in our stay. One morning, while the Ellenses were still in America, I found a disconsolate Jacob on my doorstep pointing towards an immobile lump at the far end of the garden.

"*Pugele*," he said, or at least that's what it sounded like.

"What's *pugele* Jacob?" I asked, squinting down towards the lump.

"*Woza,*" he beckoned me to "come" with him.

As we approached, I could see that the lump was the lawn mower, and that it clearly wasn't working. Jacob demonstrated its refusal to go by furiously pulling on the starter cord to no avail whatsoever. *Pugele* obviously meant something like 'broken down'. I thought I'd better find out for sure so we could put the smile back on Jacob's face. Finding Bongi hanging out the washing, I asked her to translate for me.

"*Pugele*? Is 'broken'. What you break, Missy Val?"

"Not me, Bongi, it's Jacob. He says the mower is *pugele*."

At that, she rolled her eyes expressively.

"Hah, Missy Val, it no broken. Jacob, he forget *uphethiloli.*"

She stomped off to the veranda while I mentally reprocessed what she'd said to come up with 'petrol'. Sure enough, she reappeared with a can and marched over to Jacob and the lawnmower where she berated him loudly and remorselessly as he glumly poured fuel into the tank. I felt rather sorry for him when he pulled the starting cord again and the engine roared into life. When he hastily set off again on his regular tour of the garden, I turned away. It didn't seem fair to witness his embarrassment, knowing that it could easily have been me in his position.

In fact the word *pugele*, which is actually spelt *phukile*, was one I came to know all too well in the years to come. It seemed to apply not only to things which no longer worked, but also when crockery was dropped, or the cats knocked things over, and even when the iron got too hot and burnt holes in our clothes. In short it was a useful generic term for any domestic disaster, and was by necessity delivered with a mournful shake of a knowing head. If something was *pugele*, I learnt, it was most definitely deceased.

By the time, the girls were receiving language lessons at Primary School, the segregation of schools had been thankfully outlawed, and then they had two additional languages to learn: Afrikaans and Zulu, or another African language. Neither of them attended formal schooling all the time we lived on the farm so the impact of apartheid in education did not really affect us until we left the sanctuary of our mountain.

That being said, we often saw the Zulu girls and boys on their way to school and were amazed to see that even though they had to walk miles to their lessons, and despite the fact that many of them wore no shoes, they also had a school uniform. I wondered how on earth their parents could afford it, but then it became clear that the uniform was the same for every school in the region. It seemed likely that the black sleeveless pinafore dresses worn over a white shirt by the girls and the black shorts and identical white shirts for the boys were probably quite cheap, and may well have been the most economical way of dressing the children.

Interestingly, at Richmond Primary where Jodie later went, the winter uniform was virtually the same as the Zulu children's with the exception that it was blue and not black. Coming from a background where we'd had uniforms at school which were not so strictly adhered to, I was always in trouble for my rebellious attitude to the school dress code.

Despite the stability of the dry, sunny conditions, winter mornings could be extremely cold in our part of Natal. In addition to the pinafore dresses and white shirts, there was also a school jersey and a blazer included in the winter uniform. I believed then, and still do, that if it was very cold, the children should wear both their jersey and their blazer until the sun had gained some strength and they could dispense with one or other garment as they chose.

The classrooms were housed in single storey buildings constructed on each side of a square with covered walkways giving access to each room. They had no heating and the doors were often left open to the grassed area in the centre. It was light and airy in the summer, but in the winter, my heart went out to shivering six-year olds, accustomed as they were to the cosier conditions at home.

Jodie was not a boarder, as we had moved to the Byrne valley by the time she started school and it was easy for me to take her in every day. Living at the foot of the mountain meant a quite dramatic change in climate from our elevated position on the farm. The summer was significantly hotter, and the winter proportionately colder. Having suffered a severe bout of pneumonia and pleurisy resulting from the increased extremes in temperature, I felt justified in wrapping my child up as well as possible.

Nevertheless, my rationale was not met with approval, as the school rules stated the girls could wear either their blazer or their jersey but not both. Unfortunately, obeying rules has never been my strong suit, and I contravened them shamelessly with the result that Jojo was always bringing home notes from the teacher - not about her behaviour, but mine.

Of course, these challenges were not to affect us for another year or more after Jojo's famous clangers at the farm school. In the interim, she and Mo went to play school in the mornings while I was at work, and spent their afternoons in the company of either each other or the pickannins at Bongi's kraal. Their education was informal but incredibly rich. They learnt to speak Zulu with the Kheswa clan; they learnt to read, to write and to paint with me; they dug into their own resources to invent games and a world of their own imagining, and most importantly, they learnt the ways of Africa and the laws of nature from living with it every day of their lives.

I sometimes reflect on their charmed childhood with the conviction that my daughters were blessed to live their lives there, on that mountain, in one of the most beautiful places in the natural world. I know I was.

CHAPTER 8

Elemental Hazards

When we first discussed whether to choose Canada or South Africa for our venture into the unknown, weather was an important issue, particularly for me. I wanted to be somewhere with plenty of sunshine and an average temperature equating to consistently warm. What I didn't take into account was that while rain is low on the list of drawbacks in this type of climate, it comes with others in the form of rather more acute conditions with still more extreme consequences.

I had just about got used to the severity and drama of the electric storms, and had accepted the alarming fact that more South Africans are killed by lightning than snake bites, when I was confronted by the first of a new clutch of hazards.

My first encounter with the African version of hail was during the first few months we were on the farm. I knew that there were sometimes hail storms, and we had been told often enough that the predominance of corrugated iron or 'tin' roofs in our area indicated that hail was something to be taken seriously, but I really had no clear understanding of what to expect. In Britain, we'd had occasional brisk showers of gravel sized icy particles which melted on impact. If you happened to be out in one of these outbreaks, you might feel as if you were being attacked by a swarm of cold peas and be slightly uncomfortable, but it would be nothing much to worry about. Not so in Africa.

One bright, sunny afternoon, I took the Ellenses' little Datsun *bakkie* and drove into Richmond to do some shopping. I then continued on to the sawmill to fill the *bak* of the *bakkie* with logs for the fire. There were three large forestry companies operating in Kwazulu Natal: Sappi, Mondi and HL&H, and large areas of the hills around Richmond were covered with the straight limbed wattles and pines used so extensively as pit props in the mines, and also for making into chipboard. The HL&H sawmill was just outside Richmond and as a sideline, they sold firewood to residents. However, it was not bagged up ready for collection; customers first had to drive into the yard over a weighing platform and then proceed to fill up their vehicles with as much wood as they could carry. If you hadn't brought your own help with loading, the sawmill employees would assist for the price of a decent tip. You then drove back onto the weighing machine. The difference between your entry and departure weights was calculated and this was paid for in the office before leaving. It was cheap and very fair, and I knew that the load I bought would see us through the autumn.

When I had started out that afternoon, there wasn't a cloud in the sky, but as so often happens in Natal, the weather can loom up over the Drakensberg mountains and cover the sixty or so 'crow' kilometres to Richmond within a remarkably short space of time. As I was heading back along the tar road towards the Byrne turn off, I was startled, then, to see a thick bank of what at first appeared to be rain cloud right up ahead of me. Luckily, I was travelling quite slowly due to my heavy load, so when I hit a wall of hail stones a minute or so later, both the weight in the back and my already cautious speed prevented any disasters.

It felt as if a monster tipper truck was emptying its load of ball bearings onto the *bakkie*. I couldn't see anything and the sound was deafening. Still, despite the shock of so unsolicited an attack, all I could think of was the damage it might be doing to the little pick up. It wasn't mine but I was driving it, so it was obviously going to be my fault if anything was wrong. Obviously.

Pulling cautiously to the side of the road, I waited out the storm. It didn't last long, about ten minutes at a guess, but it felt like hours while I sat in both anxiety and cacophony. When it had passed over, there was the sun again on the other side in a still, but now totally white, world. Getting out of the bakkie, I practically lost my feet from under me, as the hail stones were indeed like ball bearings. Lying a good two to three centimetres thick on the ground, they were rock hard and demonstrated absolutely no sign of melting. To describe them as small golf balls is probably exaggerating, but they were definitely considerably larger than peas, so I was relieved to see that the *bakkie* had sustained no worse damage than some chipped paint which would not be difficult to repair. My load of wood, however, looked more like a pile of ice blocks now.

Fortunately, there was nothing else on the road that day as I skated and slithered towards the Byrne turning, where after a few metres, the dirt road began. It then became easier to drive, because the hail bedded down into the mud and sand as I drove over it, and the rocks gave me some decent grip. About half way up the mountain, the road suddenly became completely dry and there was no evidence of even so much as a rain storm. I was rather disappointed. How could I now boast about my experience and bravery when I would be lucky to get anyone to believe in my hail storm to begin with? I'd forgotten about my ice blocks in the back.

Bumping over the grass towards the back entrance of our cottage, I noticed Bongi and Jacob pointing at the *bakkie* with curious expressions. I smiled to myself. My story would have some credibility after all. The smile soon faded, though, when Bongi told me with a sombre expression that it was as well I hadn't got out of the *bakkie* during the storm, or I would surely be dead. Her capacity for doom and gloom was infinitely more impressive than my tale and I felt duly deflated.

Over the following years, there were other hail storms, some still more violent, and one in particular where the soft top roof of my old, but beloved cabriolet Renault 5 looked as if it had been attacked in savage rage by a madman with a carving knife; where the stones that slashed through it were definitely the size of golf balls, and no one in possession of an iota of sense dared go outside. Nevertheless, it didn't happen all that frequently, and when it did, we just acknowledged that it was simply one of the occasional hazards of living in this normally kind and benevolent climate.

The Natal Midlands are known to be one of the areas in South Africa where tornadoes are most likely to occur. As with hail storms, they don't happen all that frequently, and often go unnoticed if their strike path encounters no built up or settled areas. In theory, though, they can occur anywhere there is a severe thunderstorm, and of course, these are an every day occurrence in the foothills of the Drakensberg.

They can also cause considerable damage, as well as loss of life in more extreme cases. As we started hearing about tornadoes, and how they are not uncommon in the Pietermaritzburg area, I realised with stirrings of concern and a mental gulp that it was one of the factors I had never considered. What's more I don't believe I had even thought of the word 'tornado' and myself in the same context. Ever. Under any circumstances.

It was consequently something of a shock to realise how close we came to being flattened by one of these devastating winds on one occasion. Given the kind of imprint it made on my mind, I'm also sure I will always know the signs if I see them again.

I was standing in the garden one afternoon, looking out to the craggy horizon of the Drakensberg when, from the north-west, I noticed a curiously yellow bunch of cloud spreading out across the sky in a kind of cyclonic form. It looked as if it had been stained with nicotine and had an unhealthy, dirty appearance. It didn't look very friendly at all. Calling to my usual fount of all meteorological wisdom, I asked Bongi what she thought it was.

She stood beside me chewing on a *mealie* cob, and I noticed with concern that she looked particularly thoughtful. She sniffed, scratched the back of her neck and then frowned. The mealie cob was suddenly directed towards me. I thought for one ludicrous moment she was going to hand it to me. Illogically distracted, I wondered how I could politely refuse her generosity in sharing this well-masticated delicacy, but then I realised she was just using it as a pointer.

"Missy Val ... look *lapa* side," (on that side) she said. The *mealie* cob turned to point in a vaguely southerly direction. Following its undulations, I eventually focused on the place in question where tell-tale dark streaks were making vertical stripes from the dense clouds into the hills beyond. Flashing forks of lightning intermittently broke through the base of the clouds to strike the earth and rocks at random. Gusts of wind were beginning to worry at the trees around us as a reminder that a storm was near.

"Well, yes I see that, Bongi, but that's normal. It's just a thunderstorm," I reasoned, marvelling that I could already be so blasé about it after years of the terrors, "but those clouds over there look different. Actually, the whole sky looks different. It's yellow!"

"That bad wind, mama, but he no come here, I think. He follow way of storm. I hope. The middle of the storm, she stay *lapa* side." The *mealie* cob again directed my attention to the hills ahead.

I didn't really know what she meant, and I was a bit troubled by the simple "I hope". It seemed to rely a bit more on faith than the confidence I would have preferred. Nonetheless, we carried on about our business, and only occasionally did I look uneasily outside whenever an unusually strong gust of wind made the roof rattle or the dust clouds sweep across the garden. The yellow sky continued to trawl across the valleys ahead of us.

Later that evening, as the wind increased in strength and rain pounded at the windows, we heard on the radio that late in the afternoon, a tornado had torn through a valley about fifteen kilometres distant, uprooting trees, shacks and houses. It had picked up both cows and sheep and hurled them like weightless balls through the air, killing them with its savagery. Still worse, it had tossed a *bakkie* and its driver a hundred and fifty metres into the *veld*, ripping out its engine in the process. Needless to say, the poor driver did not survive.

Shuddering at what had thankfully passed us by, I listened to the full extent of what a tornado can do. The radio reporter was graphic in his description. The destruction was horrific, and it was a sobering thought to realise that this had just been a small one. I learnt too that the yellow sky was the effect of dust being whipped up into the atmosphere and held there by the centrifugal forces of the wind. It was indeed dirty and stained and its image has remained indelibly printed on my memory.

However, wind is still more an enemy to be reckoned with when accompanied by fire. Most countries with areas of continental climate experience bush fires and forest fires of one kind or another, and so are no strangers to the horrors and fear of flames whipped up by wind. It is probably no surprise then to know that *veld* fires are a seasonal hazard in South Africa in most parts of the country, and particularly in those areas which have no winter rainfall.

The months from April through to September are always dry in Natal, and so the grass shrivels to the brittleness of bleached straw. As winter progresses, everything becomes brown and parched except for the trees. The risk of fire, either accidental or deliberate, is a perennial anxiety. At Cottingham, as on every other farm in the region, the owner Tony made fire-breaks when the grasses became too dry. These are wide stretches about five metres across and extending down the sides of the fields which are burnt under controlled conditions. That way, if a runaway fire should take hold, the pre-burnt sections could do much to prevent it spreading further.

Firebreak time is quite fun for the farming community as it often involves team efforts accompanied by braais, beer and lots of brawn. Jokes fly and anyone who happens to be bald inevitably gets teased about standing in the way of the firebreak team. It is hot dirty work, so good humour is a requirement of the job, but the serious intent with which it is carried out is no joke at all. On each side of the designated firebreak, the burning party sets light to the grass using an accelerant or blow torch, and moves down the line of the field. They are then followed by a beater or two whose job is to extinguish the flames after making sure everything between the two sidelines is burnt. Concentration is needed, as there is always a risk of the fire escaping, especially if there is any kind of breeze blowing.

Some other friends of ours, an Englishman and his wife, lived in an old thatched farm house on their sixty odd acres in the valley. They grew a bit of everything, but their crop fields didn't extend far from the house which was ringed by tall wattle trees. Beyond these there were sweeping pastures of yellow *veld* grass that belonged to a neighbouring farmer. We were spending an afternoon with them one winter weekend, enjoying the obligatory *braai* in their shady garden when their farmhand came rushing in.

"Fire, sah, fire!" He panted, as he almost skidded to a halt in front of our host's chair.

It would have been comical if it hadn't been so alarming. Our friend shot out of his chair and went pelting off with his foreman, while his wife immediately, and with great presence of mind, armed all her guests with sticks, brooms or sheets of fabric that could be wetted and used to beat out the flames if necessary.

All of us trooped off to the edge of their lands to see where the danger was coming from. Sure enough, over one of the fields of long, dry, winter grass, flames were gathering pace, urged on by the force of a brisk wind.

As the wind picked up, so did the flames and it wasn't long before they were three to four metres high, sending out sparks which reached several metres higher. The roaring sound was terrifying as it built up in strength and volume. It seemed so relentless and so inevitable, a conflagration the width of two football fields, leaping, thundering and spitting its way towards us with searing, burning, hellish breath. All we could do at that stage was watch and wait, and pray to all our collective Gods that the firebreaks would do the job.

Suddenly, the sparks began to shoot still higher, and although we knew the flames would be arrested in their path, we could see that the wattles were in danger of catching fire. Despite the fact that their needles remained green, they were also dried out from the parched conditions, and would catch light easily given the heat of the burning particles.

This would be a disaster. The trees were too close by far for the thatched roof of the house to escape danger, and even as we discussed what to do, the first branches caught alight. Then someone, or maybe everyone, had the same idea. Find as many hosepipes as possible, turn them on to the roof and soak it through. It was amazing really. Amidst the panic, there was a coolness and collective approach to the calamity that turned the entire proceedings into a military drill. We moved through our paces, collected hosepipes, found connectors, attached them to taps, and from several different vantage points sprayed the thatched roof of the house mercilessly.

Every now and then, someone went inside to check whether water was seeping through, and sure enough it was, but fortunately there were no plaster ceilings to worry about, as the house was open to the roof. Consequently, we all agreed that water damage to furnishings was a small price to pay in exchange for saving their home.

Eventually, the fire did indeed burn itself out against the breaks, and the hoses were then turned onto the smouldering branches of the wattle trees, which in due course also fizzled out to leave a pungent and acrid smelling smoke.

By this time, it was quite late in the evening, and what had been a pleasant afternoon's *braai* had transmogrified into a nightmarish hell from which we were all relieved to escape. There was only one thing for it. Festivities were resumed in good South African tradition.

Beer cans were popped, the wine carton was broached once more, and we all sat back out in the garden. It must have been a curious sight. A dozen or so blackened individuals, all reeking of wet smoke, but all laughing and talking as if nothing had occurred to interrupt their social conviviality. Nevertheless, a keen observer might have noticed a slightly hysterical pitch to the laughter and a more than usually expressive quality to the tone of the voices. If so, that person would probably have been right. The sheer relief of overcoming the most frightening of all the elements had made us all a little over enthusiastic about life that night, regardless of the odd and distinctly filthy state of our appearance. We weren't about to let the occasion go unnoticed in any event, so a little extra zest was hardly surprising in the circumstances.

Not all elemental hazards have to do with the weather, although I suppose it depends on how you define elemental. In our case, I've extended its meaning to include other things natural and in this particular instance, to bees. Some people are violently allergic to nature's honey producers, but on the whole we tend to regard them as fairly benign creatures with many a children's tale including them in their cast of personified animal characters. I was among those that bore a kindly attitude to the bee and had always been at pains not to kill them. There are circumstances, however, where they can take on a more alarming face, and although our experience was not unique to Africa, it happened to us on the farm because of the structure of the old colonial style homestead.

The little room the girls shared was actually part of the old house, but had been included into our later-built cottage to provide an extra bedroom. It was, in fact, a closed-in section of the back veranda and had a door leading directly out onto the covered area. As a result, it had rather less solid foundations than the house itself, added to which there were several air bricks in its base to allow for ventilation.

When Mo was still in her cot, and not yet walking, she often stood holding on to the railings pointing at the odd bee that buzzed around on the inside of the cottage pane windows. In her turn, Jojo tried her best to teach her baby sister to talk, and before long she learnt to say 'bee' with great conviction and aplomb. It was her first word, and I suppose I should have had a premonition about this. Normal children usually learn something like "mama" or "papa" before they learn about birds and bees.

However, I wasn't too worried about it. Bees were indeed fact of life, and there were always a few around, attracted by the wealth of flowering shrubs in Oupa's garden. They didn't bother us as long as we too left them alone. I didn't even get concerned when the one or two bees multiplied to four or five. It was early spring and these things were to be expected.

The day came, though, when I walked into my daughters' room, and there were bees flying everywhere. Mo was sitting in her cot holding a small wriggling yellow and black striped object between two fingers. She proudly held it out to me and said "bee" very firmly and positively. I gasped and gulped simultaneously. The next thing that happened was that she let go of the bee which promptly and understandably got its own back for the indignity she had served on it by stinging her just below her right eye.

Without further hesitation, I scooped up my baby and retreated rapidly, closing the door on an image of bees zooming and buzzing happily round the room. What did one do about bee stings? I had some vague recollection of calamine lotion, but after scouring my bathroom cupboard, it was clear I had nothing in the way of medicines other than an ancient tube of acne cream. Somehow, I couldn't see this being very helpful against a fresh and virulent bee sting.

Within half an hour, Mo's eye had swollen to a red-rimmed blue-encircled lump and I realised that anyone with a tendency to be critical could have been forgiven for thinking I had hit her. I was thankful I didn't have to go anywhere for a day or two, but then I hadn't reckoned on the protective instincts of a Bongi.

When she saw my little one with her impressive black eye, she snatched her away from me and started a one-

Bongi diatribe on the wickedness of my negligent behaviour.

"How missy Val! What you do? Why you leave Momo? *Woza* Mo, come, *umama omubi* your mama, she very bad! *Kanjani*? How you do that? *Hamba* missy Val! You go, Momo stay with me!" She was really very cross indeed.

The good news was that it never occurred to her that I'd hit Mo, but she clearly thought I'd left her alone and unprotected, and that she'd caught her eye on something hard in a fall.

I'd found before that interrupting Bongi in mid-flow was only likely to increase the force and length of her outburst, so instead of attempting to explain, I led her, still spouting an incomprehensible mixture of Zulu and garbled English, to the girls' bedroom and opened the door.

Her mouth gaped open, but then so did mine. The whole room was swarming with bees. We slammed the door closed quickly and hastily retreated to the kitchen. Luckily, there were two steps up into the children's room, and the door closed against the bottom step, making a good seal against the bees' possible infiltration into the rest of the flat.

As far as I know, bees only swarm once a year in England, but apparently, they can and do more frequently in Africa. On this occasion, it was quite early in the spring, and what made things worse was the drought with its consequent higher temperatures. The bees were busy looking for cosy places to get down and make honey rather sooner than they would normally do. It seemed too that this colony had decided that my children's room was just the ticket for a warm, cosy hive.

Rather perplexed about what to do, and conscious that it was quite dangerous to argue with a determined bunch of busy bees, I went to seek Oupa Ellens's advice, together with Bongi who was still carrying the evidence of the bees' villainy. Mo seemed rather un-phased by her black eye, and only too happy to be receiving all this unsolicited attention, and so greeted her Oupa with a comic grin and outstretched arms.

"Well now," he quipped, "who have you been in the ring with little one, your sister, hmm?"

"A swarm of very inhospitable bees, Willem," I cut in. "In her bedroom. And what's worse, they seem to have no intention of leaving."

"Ohhhh, they're back are they?" He had the grace to look a bit sheepish." They were there last Christmas, just before you came, but I thought we'd got rid of them. They aren't in the room itself," he explained. "They make their hive under the floor because they can get through that air brick below the window. It's mostly hollow under there, because it used to be part of the veranda."

One of the most important warnings bee keepers will give you, if you have a problem such as this, is that once you have eradicated the hive, you must clear out all of the remaining honey comb and detritus of the former bee population. Failure to do this, they say sternly, will encourage the scouts to come looking the next time around, and ultimately bring the entire swarm. This, it appeared, is exactly what had happened. The time to take action was now, before they started making their new honeycomb on the foundations of the old.

That night, we moved enough of the girls' possessions out of the room while the bees were sleeping. It felt rather odd, creeping about as if we were afraid of waking a monster, but Bill and I certainly felt very uneasy and tiptoed through our tasks, just whispering when communication was necessary. We made two extra beds up in our room, and were soon tucking in two small girls, whose excitement at changing rooms couldn't even have been exceeded by prospects of a holiday at the beach.

The following morning, before the sun was really up and while the bees were still snoozing, two veiled and totally overalled individuals waddled round the back of the house carrying the tools of Bee Mansions' potential demolition. It was impossible to tell who was who, but I knew it was Willem and Jacob. I also knew that their methods were going to be rather primitive. They intended to smoke the bees out and drive them away rather than kill them. I preferred this idea to killing them with a gas that wouldn't only decimate the swarm itself, but might also be harmful to us.

The windows to the small bedroom were opened wide, while all the other windows in the house were firmly closed. Where there were air bricks and gaps, we had all teamed up to tape them over. It felt as if we were preparing for a siege. Bill then went off to work, and the girls, Bongi, Ouma and I shut ourselves in the main bedroom and watched the proceedings with trepidation.

Our window was at right-angles to the wall where the bees had found their way in, so we had a cinematic view of what our extermination crew were doing. The two swaddled figures that were Oupa and Jacob in another life, prepared bunches of sticks and bound them tightly together. They then set light to the bunches, and as soon as they were burning properly, the flames were extinguished and the smouldering, smoking ends pushed into the hole that the bees had used as an entrance. This continued until the hole was totally jammed with the sticks. Although it seemed as if time had slowed to a standstill, it wasn't really long before we saw trails of smoke coming out of the bedroom window, suggesting that this somewhat basic method was doing its job. Shortly after this, bedlam began in Bee Mansions.

The two human destroyers signalled to each other and withdrew to the relative safety of the veranda just as the first bees shot out of the little bedroom windows. Moments later, a mass exodus started, and the swarm poured out of the room, looking for all the world like something from a sci-fi horror movie. They spread out in a huge cloud in front of our window and milled around, seeming confused and directionless. Despite the comprehensive cover of their protective clothing, Willem and Jacob huddled together against the wall as the bees circled them angrily. Then suddenly, they found a different focus, and as one pulled together into a cohesive form and flew off towards the tress. I guessed the Queen had finally given them the order to march, and they set out to find another, more welcoming abode.

During the entire process, not one of us had said a word, but as we watched the swarm disappear round some dense bushes, there was an audible exhalation of breath as we all relaxed.

"Now," began Ouma Ellens with a steely resolve in her eye, "Jacob must take out the floor in that room, and clear it out properly this time."

Aha, I thought to myself, so she had also guessed what had happened. I could well imagine it. After the last bee episode, Willem and Jacob had probably teamed up against her and tried to convince her that it would be all right; that the bees wouldn't come back; that they would fill in the holes so they couldn't come back. But it hadn't happened that way. The airbrick was left open, and the smell of the old honeycomb and probably a few dozen dead bees had acted as a magnet for a new hive.

There was no escaping the tedious duty this time though. Over the next few days, Jacob was pulled off gardening duty, which he loved, and put on the floor-dismantling job, which he didn't. As a result, every time I saw him resting on his tools, looking as if he would like to take in a bit of slack time, I hoisted Mo with her nicely purple and black eye into my arms and went to check on his progress. It only took one look at my poor innocent and bruised child before he got the message.

CHAPTER 9

High Days And Holidays

When you live in heaven, where do you go for a holiday? Or for a day out? I'm sure the average celestial resident doesn't have such concerns, but from our very first day at Cottingham, we knew we would never live anywhere as idyllic ever again. The question of leaving our mountain, then, even for a weekend break, was quite a dilemma for us 'imports'. There was still so much of the country to be seen. On the other hand, the temptation to sit back, vegetate in our private universe and dismiss the rest of South Africa, and the world as well, was not just idle fancy. It really was an effort to motivate ourselves to go anywhere beyond our usual sphere of activity.

At normal weekends, there was of course the usual shopping to be done. This in itself could be an adventure, albeit a regular one. We generally had a three-stop routine: during the week, I would buy the minor daily needs from Asmal's. Then on Fridays, I went into Richmond and shopped for our weekly needs.

Richmond was described in my tourist guide as a 'charming village', but I never quite figured out where the author had gone to find the charm, as it was exceptionally well hidden. My first impression of the town was of a run down and haphazard collection of buildings without much rhyme and very little reason. It was built around a crossroads, which had a garage on one corner, a shabby and peeling bottle store on its opposite site, the colourful Bridgeway Stores diagonally across from it and a faded but pretty colonial building housing a haberdashers and wool shop on the fourth corner. As I said, no reason – or at least no cohesion – apart from the four-way stop.

I did most of my shopping at Bridgeway Stores, which was like an upmarket trading store, as it was laid out in a conventional style with aisles and shelves in some kind of logical order. In short, it was a stack-and-pack supermarket with practically everything you could possibly wish to buy except fresh fruit and vegetables; that is fruit and vegetables that really showed some semblance of having been harvested within our lifetime. For these and the other more vulnerable and perishable food stuffs, I went to Sizanani which was the closest thing we had to a modern food store.

Formerly a Spar supermarket, Sizanani was clean, airy and smart, although even here, there was that faint, but penetrating aroma of meat past its 'eat me' date, condition normal in these warmer climes. It was located at the bottom of a hill on the edge of town, and came as a surprise after the rows of ramshackle old shops with decaying columns and rusty tin roofs that lined the street leading down from the crossroads. Sizanani breathed 'suburbia' and always seemed to me to be a bit out of place in our backwoods settlement. Surprisingly, the residential areas that backed up to the two main streets were very pleasant, and had low sprawling bungalows with exuberant gardens, sheltering behind their tree lined streets. Unfortunately, though, they were too well concealed to alter the first impression, which was of course the one that lasted.

Nevertheless, Richmond was thriving and colourful, even if it was shabby, and I enjoyed my trips into town to stock up on essentials. Apart from the usual provisions, the round normally included picking up twenty litres of paraffin for our lamps and fridge, or a bottle of gas for the cooker or geyser, all of which were available at Bridgeway stores. Then, a dive into the bottle store to collect a few crates of beer along with the standard five litre box of wine, and in winter, a visit to the sawmill to fetch a load of logs. It was a self-sufficient lifestyle, but still dependent on buying the raw materials for our survival rather than producing them ourselves. I relished that feeling of bulk buying, though, as it had a feel of real life lived in serious quantities.

The third stop was the great Saturday trek into Pietermaritzburg. We didn't do this every week, as it wasn't always necessary, with the result that it felt like quite an occasion when we drove in *en famille*.

The drive along the R56 took about forty minutes to cover the sixty odd kilometres into the provincial capital. The road was a good, mostly three lane highway which rolled over undulating hills, and between green carpeted fields whose resemblance to pastoral England was enhanced by signposts to villages with the chronically English names of Thornville and Baynesfield.

Pietermaritzburg lies in a dip surrounded by hills, and is affectionately known as the 'sleepy hollow'. Owing to its geographical location, it can get extremely hot in the city centre, with the temperature rising to heights that would be unusual beyond its surrounding hills. However, it buzzed with life on Saturdays and holidays.

Entering the city was always a pleasure because it appeared to be permanently bustling with a lively and mixed throng of people. Students, families and grannies from every sector of South Africa's rainbow hued nation clogged the shaded sidewalks, and moved, shoal-like in and out of department stores and clothing outlets. Cafés spilled onto the pavements with Saturday morning breakfasters, and the aroma of good coffee wafted tantalisingly on the air. We always succumbed to the temptation.

We had a favourite coffee bar which did a mouth-watering breakfast of bacon, mushroom and cheese baguettes. They were stuffed so full, we could barely force our jaws open wide enough to take a bite let alone prevent the contents from squishing out the sides, while the combined flavours soaked into the fresh, crisp bread to create a taste of sheer and utter heaven. Coffee was a 'bottomless cup', meaning that you could keep going back for re-fills without extra charge, and if you wanted milk with it, it was always hot and frothy. It was just divine, and was a treat we looked forward to with relish.

With hunger and taste buds satisfied, we went to shop for the things we couldn't buy in Richmond, such as clothes and luxury items. We savoured our shopping sprees and took our time, weaving our way along the crowded pavements with all the other locals. There was the music shop where I bought my first guitar and where we later bought banjos, music being our substitute for television in the evenings. Then came department stores, which despite their size were situated in the main shopping streets, and wore their names in huge garish signs: Game, Dion's, Woolworths; they were all there in the heart of the old city, and not, as is found in so many urban areas, confined to modern out-of-town shopping malls.

I pushed the girls through the crowds in a 'twin buggy', my handy pushchair for two. The aisles in the stores were wide so this worked quite well as it kept them under control – that is until the day I found Momo munching a chocolate bar she had lifted from a lower shelf in passing. Trying to persuade a one and a bit year old that shoplifting is frowned upon, even for those below the age of conscience, let alone reason, was fruitless, so the buggy had to be replaced by a baby backpack.

The charm of Natal at that period was that although we were still living under apartheid, there was thankfully little visible evidence of it, even in Pietermaritzburg. The contrast between the living conditions of the affluent and the poor was of course tragically noticeable, but that is true of the big cities in most parts of the world apart from Europe and North America. However, in the centre of 'Maritzburg, the legalised segregation of the races was not as evident as it was in, say, Johannesburg. Shoppers mingled and queued for the same goods in the same rows, and black, white and Asian mothers carried babies on backs, fronts and hips through the same crowds. It was a cheerful, vibrant environment of which I was happy to be a part, and I mourned the change when the consequences of political unrest threw this friendly city into disarray and neglect.

A morning in 'Maritzburg always passed quickly, so sometimes, we stayed for lunch as well. On the way out of town, there was a restaurant-cum-bakery unimaginatively called the "Bake and Take", but the décor was rustic with charm, and displayed no shortage of creativity. It also had tables on a wooden deck facing the road but shaded by large spreading Jacaranda trees, so it was a pleasant place to sit and relax and watch the world go by after the morning's activity.

Being quite close to the university, it was popular with students as somewhere to eat as well as to work, so Bake and Take could be relied upon to be both cheap and cheerful. It was also very good, and the pies, pastries and sandwiches they produced on the premises were completely delectable. Finishing our trip here was a satisfying close to the shopping excursion, but it was just as likely to be a close to the day as well. After the typically South African generosity of the portions of pies, salads and fries, accompanied by creamy milkshakes, and followed by rich aromatic coffee, we often arrived home only to collapse and sleep till sunset.

However, I digress. Shopping excursions hardly fall into the category of days out or holidays as most people would understand them, even if they were greeted with the same enthusiasm by my family. These aside, there were some other memorable trips that were marked by either their beauty, or simply their fun value, or in one instance by its sheer lunacy.

Into the former fell a drive to the Sani Pass, the Drakensberg mountain border post with the Kingdom of Lesotho. Making our way up the twisting, rocky dirt road to the summit of the pass, and to then stand at such a remote border post with another country in the sharp clarity of the winter sunshine, was in itself so special that I'm sure I can still smell the arid air and feel the keenness of the wind even today. Add to this the pleasure of watching two small children splashing through mountain streams, oblivious of the icy temperature, and seeing the sun set behind a snow-tipped peak, and you have a set of marvellous recollections to carry with you through a lifetime.

Into the fun category went several trips to the Midmar or Albert Falls dams to meet friends with boats and water skis, to *braai*, to mess about in the water and go home as the light sunk below the hills, warm with sun, tired out with fun and basking in the glow of friendships re-affirmed.

As for the episode of sheer lunacy, this occurred one bright autumn Saturday. We had been listening to Capitol, a radio station which claimed to broadcast from the town of Port St John's, a settlement on the Wild Coast in the Transkei, which at that time was a separate homeland for which we needed passports to enter. The DJ's played the normal mix of Top Twenty hits, but somehow the fact that they were playing them from what seemed to us to be an almost illicit tropical paradise, gave the station an extra allure and glamour. I had mental centrefolds of tanned, golden young men, barely dressed, sitting behind turntables in a beachside hut against a setting of dazzling white sands and indigenous bush. I suspect that Bill was imagining the same vision in female form with the dress even more minimal. We didn't compare notes, but curiously we both had the same compulsion to go and see if our fantasy was matched by reality.

That Saturday, the skies were a limitless blue and the air was fresh with the promise of adventure. It was a day for impulse, and we succumbed. Packing two still sleepy children into the back of our little red Ford, we set off with a route description, having calculated that it was about two hundred kilometres to Transkei's capital, Umtata. How wrong we were was made clear when we arrived in

Umtata close to four hundred kilometres and several hours later.

It had become a mission of determination and endurance by that time. The drive to the border post had been accompanied by 'oohs and aahs' of appreciation for the splendour and lushness of the vegetation. We'd stopped at Kokstad for toasties and milkshakes, and cheerfully continued on our optimistic way. Some time later, we'd exhausted our ability to 'ooh' and looking at each other guiltily, realised we'd long since passed the two-hundred-kilometre mark.

The first inkling of what was to develop into nonsensical hysteria was when I realised I'd left my passport behind, and I didn't have my ID book either. The girls were in Bill's passport, so that was no problem, but after travelling so far, we were totally set on reaching our goal. Just before the border post, we stopped and Bill gave me his ID book, suggesting we just chance it. We both had short dark hair and I was wearing dark glasses, so if I put my thumb over the first name, and just shoved the page in front of the immigration officer, we might just get away with it. Much to our relief, the border post was poorly manned that Saturday morning, and the officer in charge asked Bill to fill in a form for all of us instead of the usual individual papers. Nevertheless, we all had to go inside the immigration hall, a long featureless and hot room with a single scarred wooden counter dividing it down its length. Ceiling fans swished lethargically round, and as we waited for him to process our form, the silence seemed to weigh down on me like a suffocating mantle. I was dreading our imminent expulsion.

Then I became transfixed by a fly buzzing round the officer's bald pink head which he swotted absentmindedly. The fly of course levitated, buzzed a quick lap round the room, and settled back on exactly the same spot until the performance was repeated. Every now and then, the officer would lick his finger, scratch his head where the fly had been busy doing what flies do and then lick his finger again. I was morbidly and totally fascinated. In the meantime my palms were sweating with anxiety, and my mouth was dry.

When it came to showing him our travel documents, I could barely open my mouth, as my lips were glued together with dried up saliva. To my amazement, though, he gave no more than a lazy glance at the photos, took one speculative look at me, wrote down the numbers and handed them back. He never even checked the names against the forms. During this whole exchange, the officer had not said a word. He had grunted, pointed, hummed and sniffed, and somehow managed to convey what was required to us without opening his mouth. At the same time, whether or not it was intended, he had also managed to be fearfully intimidating.

Swallowing for the first time since we had entered the building, we filed out into the sunshine and got back into our car. A few yards further on, a Transkei border control officer, peered inside to check us through. His round smooth face was split with a grin the size of a melon slice as he cheerfully welcomed us to his homeland. It was all the warmth and encouragement we needed to pursue our quest rather than turn tail and go home.

Bill showed him the stamped and authorised form, which he matched to the bodies in the car and with that, he lifted the boom and waved us through. At last, I let out a whoop of relief. I couldn't believe we'd got away with it, and indeed the tale of how I became 'wo-man' for the day was a long laughed over story for years to come.

The road from the border to Umtata was such a contrast to the South African side from which we had come that we were quickly sobered by the reality of what the homelands really meant to the people who were obliged to live in them. The land was devastatingly eroded with barely a blade of grass to be seen and just a hint of green staining the red surface of the cracked and pitted fields. The surface was full of potholes; goats and cattle wandered across at will with the consequent messy results left to rot where they had been dispatched. It was a grim and stark reminder of the poverty that accompanied these people every day of their lives. Villages were dilapidated groups of shacks with a matching trading store at best. Water was clearly scarce and women could be seen on every stretch of road, carrying containers aloft. Who knows how many kilometres they would have to walk to find this basic essential of life.

Umtata itself was shabby, bustling, colourful and dirty, rather like a large scale Richmond, but we had no time to stop. By now we were in a mood of desperate fortitude. We would make it to Port St Johns if it killed us. We'd left before eight in the morning, and it was already early afternoon. Indeed, the worst part of the journey was still to come.

As we left the city heading towards the coast, we noticed the road deteriorating still further. The girls, who had been astonishingly patient and well behaved so far, started to grizzle plaintively with every lurch and bump and even I began to grit my teeth to prevent myself from groaning with frustration. After some distance and quite suddenly, we arrived at the great metropolis of Lusikisiki. At least,

144

this was the feeling conveyed. It was announced with a huge notice board welcoming us expansively. A further large sign directed the 'through traffic' to other routes in one direction and the centre to the right, so at this point we started looking around to see what all the fuss was about.

We saw The Great Stadium – a large bare field with a couple of posts at each end. A banner announced The Airport up ahead. This turned out to be a well trampled track up the centre of a bumpy meadow. We were terribly impressed. Not by the extent of the facilities, naturally, but more by the sheer optimism and exuberance of the confidence displayed. We began to join the spirit of the thing and when we saw a tiny building next to a railway line, it immediately became Grand Central Station, while the wattle and daub hut that boasted the police post assumed the mantle of the Palais de Justice. Maybe it was a touch of hysteria arising from the ludicrous adventure on which we had embarked, but by the time we regretfully left the worthy environs of Lusikisiki, we were crying with laughter and the two infants in the back were silent with either disapproval or dismay; we weren't quite sure which.

From here on, the tar road was no more and the remaining fifty odd kilometres to Port St John's were undertaken on a gravel track whose condition dwindled with every passing milepost. The laughter evaporated with the tears, and we wound up our windows to protect ourselves from the swirling dust created by the series of rattling *bakkies*, ancient cars and buses-pulling-trailers that belted past us with no concession to the legal principle of driving on the left. Indeed it seemed that everyone in this part of the world must have been instructed on their inalienable right of way along the middle of the road, on the premise that anyone else was required to give way to

145

them automatically. The debris of unresolved disputes littered the bank that dropped away from the road – a sorry reminder of the consequences of proud intransigence.

Our little car hugged bends round mountain passes overlooking stretching tea plantations. Citrus orchards climbed the rocky hillsides in serried ranks, and the landscape became increasingly tropical in its vegetation and flora. Despite the cultivation, however, there appeared to be no sign of human habitation, and although we occasionally saw individuals walking along the side of the road, we couldn't imagine where they had come from or where they were heading.

Eventually, the road began to drop down. As we wound our way down to the valleys, we began to see what we had missed before. Groups of thatched *rondavels* clustered in small clearings but were so thickly surrounded by the plantations and orchards, we hadn't noticed them from our aerial view. Still, it could hardly be called densely populated, and at no point did we see a shop, so the poor residents must have walked tens of kilometres to buy any of the supplies they couldn't grow or make themselves. Before we reached the valley floor, the road became little better than a collection of ruts, held together by rocks. It had obviously rained heavily quite recently and the best part of the surface had been washed away. It was a murderous descent from which we all emerged with somewhat ragged nerves and bruised behinds.

To be on the flat was blissful relief, and after driving for some time through thick indigenous bush with great towering trees on either side, we were joined by a slinky silent river which ran parallel to our road, and which widened noticeably as the valley deepened into a huge gorge. It was the great Umzimvubu, which ended its journey at Port St John's and we knew that, at last, we were reaching our goal. Then suddenly and without warning the road transformed itself into a tarred town street, and white painted houses began to be visible among the trees. We'd made it. Four hundred and plenty more kilometres of tough, concentrated driving it had been, but we had definitely arrived. Our goal achieved.

The question now was what to do next. We cruised gently into the town's centre and were charmed by the old world colonial style of the gracefully decaying buildings. It was like something out of Casablanca or a movie set in the Havana of the fifties. Bougainvillea bushes spilled their flowers over garden walls and flame trees splashed colour with vermillion vibrancy along the roadside. The whole town was dazzling in its contrasts of greens, white and all the clashing reds of a sub tropical paradise. An old hotel of fading grandeur basked on its sunlit corner and indeed the whole town appeared to be asleep as nothing much moved except perhaps the odd cat sloping languidly from one place of comfort to the next.

We headed for the beach by following the Umzimvubu river until it opened its mouth into a bay of quite astonishing beauty. The sands were virtually white with the bay an almost perfect semi circle against the backdrop of dense vegetation that covered the steep hillsides. In the far corner of the beach, a small colonial style house nestled amongst the trees, and my heart instantly yearned to be left here in this paradise. The sky was a relentless steely blue, and the autumn sun glowed on our aching muscles, penetrating and healing. This area of shoreline is known as the Wild Coast, due to its reputation for violent and damaging storms, but that day it couldn't have looked more tranquil. The usually restless ocean was calm and inviting as it rippled across the silken sands.

The beach was completely empty with one exception. Drawing shapes in its smooth surface with a long, finely fashioned walking stick was a beautiful Xhosa boy of around fourteen years old. As we approached, he greeted us solemnly, so we decided to ask him if he knew where we could find some lunch. He looked at us patiently with his wide, clear eyes.

"What you like to eat, sir, madam? There are three places in the village. You say me, Sobriety will show you."

"Sobriety?" Bill asked curiously

"Sobriety my name, sir," he said proudly, and I could just imagine him spending his days trying to live up to so worthy a calling. He really was so very beautiful with his clear-eyed innocence that the rather puritanical solemnity with which he addressed us and spoke gave him a rather quaint and old-fashioned air.

We decided to follow suit and after a seriously considered discussion in which the children also played along, Bill told him rather formally what we would like.

"Well, Sobriety, the small madams desire chips and milkshakes, while the big madam and I would enjoy the same as we are no larger than the small madams at heart."

Sobriety's face broke into a huge grin of sheer delight.

"Is sir joking with Sobriety?"

"Sir is indeed, and if Sobriety will show us where we may eat like the small madams without shame, we shall be forever grateful," Bill finished with a small bow.

Our new guide was totally delighted with us and immediately hoisted Mo onto his back and took Jojo by the hand before leading us to a guest house on the far end of the town quay. It was an unassuming looking place, but they served us with burgers, chips and milkshakes with as much grease and synthetic colouring as anywhere else in the country, so all in all everyone was happy and much refreshed after the long arduous journey.

When we came out, Sobriety was waiting for us. He was sitting on the wall of the quay, staring out into the bay with the same stillness we had noticed in him earlier. I felt very drawn to this boy who seemed to have such a capacity for inner peace. He led us back to the beach and took us to the northern end where there were great slabs of rock with little pools full of sea anemones, small crabs and tiny sea creatures we had never seen before. He then led us across the cliffs to a second beach which was wilder and even more beautiful than the first, and lastly he showed us a cliff path where flowers and grasses grew of so rich a variety that I wished I had some means of identifying them.

As the sun turned from white hot to golden glow, we realised regretfully that we had better be starting back. We didn't really want to be on the dirt road after dark, given the unpredictable nature of the oncoming traffic.

Bidding Sobriety a sorry farewell, we offered him a R10 note for his exceptional devotion to duty, which he accepted modestly without even looking to see what it was. In customary style, he held the wrist of his outstretched hand with his other hand and bowed his head in thanks. We promised we would return. We did. Frequently.

As it happened, after the magical discovery of this trip, we mostly took our holidays in Port St John's during the years we lived in Natal. It complemented our mountain kingdom perfectly in its tropical splendour. Sometimes we went with friends, sometimes alone. We camped at the municipal site in tents or stayed in the self catering *rondavels*; we paid the local pickannins to dive from the rocks and catch crayfish for us and cooked them on the moonlit beach. We walked the cliff tops and found further inlets, caves and coves. The local shops provided us with all our somewhat basic needs, and it was almost perfect. But although we looked and waited, we never saw our Sobriety again. Somewhere, though, I still have a photo of that beautiful boy, standing on the gleaming sands of the beach in his solitary splendour.

Our return journey that evening was rather silent as we absorbed the experiences of the day and did our best to endure the discomforts of the roads. Bill and I took turns with the driving, so we could have breaks, and the girls slept practically all the way back after the light had finally dipped below the horizon. At the border, I feigned sleep as the official on duty checked us back through, merely making sure that the individuals who had left that morning were the same ones returning, and we carried on home with no further ado.

By the time we arrived back on the farm, it was around 12.30. The trip had taken us about six hours each way, and we'd had just over four hours in Port St John's. We knew it was crazy, but we'd had a wonderful day. And then, we agreed, if you already live in one part of heaven, a hellish road trip may be the only way to appreciate the beauty of one of its other parts. The real irony only occurred to us the following day when we turned on our radio. We had gone all that way to see the base from which our favourite station was broadcast, but far from seeing any bronzed hunks turning discs and flouting convention, we hadn't even given them a thought or seen any evidence of their existence. We'd been far too occupied with our Sobriety.

CHAPTER 10

What It All Comes Down To In The End

By 1984, we had been living on the farm for three years, and for myself, I would have been content to stay there indefinitely. Bill, however, was more ambitious, and with his new high-profile job in Durban came increased travelling and greater demands on his free time. The drive up the rocky road to the farm didn't disturb him, but having somewhere of our own to entertain visitors was becoming an issue, not to mention the desire to start building up some assets in the country ourselves.

After much discussion and agonising, we decided to look for a small house to buy in the area, so that at least I could maintain the social contacts I had built around myself and the children. This was really a compromise and ultimately proved to be the wrong choice, but as these things do, it seemed like a good idea at the time.

The result was that we moved out of the farm cottage late in November, 1984 and during several *bakkie* and car trips, hauled our accumulated possessions down the mountain to the village of Byrne, nestled in the valley. Our new home was a charming white cottage with leaded diamond pane windows and a slate roof. We had half an acre of garden with fruit trees galore and space enough for the children to play all the hide-and-seek games they could possibly invent. We were naturally very excited about our new home, and we threw ourselves into the task of making it our own.

But, and this is an important but, it was the end of an era. We thought we would continue to go up the winding track and visit the farm regularly, but we didn't. We thought our lives wouldn't alter all that much, but they did, and we thought we would be even happier now that we had a place that was really our own, but we weren't. However, this is not part of this story or indeed this book, as it ultimately led to other changes which took us away from Kwazulu Natal completely.

But I digress. Looking back through the anecdotes and stories written here, the focus of the attention has been on the affection we developed for the people who lived on and around the farm. In retrospect, what still seems to be missing is the series of images that remain with me whenever I think of the life we led there, so it feels fitting that I should end this collection of tales with a sort of 'round up' of the enduring impressions and feelings about our mountain 'years' that live with me to this day.

So it is that the next pages are devoted to those daily experiences that left their stamp on my life. They also include such intangibles as atmosphere, scents, light and reflection. They are the full and glorious technicolour imprints in my mind, and I hope they convey some of the sense of wonder and pleasure that I still feel when I think back to that remote corner of the world I was so very fortunate to call home for a short spell of time.

Lighting up time

There are no long days in Natal. Even at the height of summer, the evening fades into darkness quite rapidly at around seven o'clock, the result of being at a latitude south of the equator similar to that of Cairo to its north.

Living in a world without electricity steered us into century-old routines which have their own form of gentle, timeless ritual, and lighting the oil lamps was a daily practice whose timing didn't alter too much from winter to summer. It was a task I savoured, even though I always put it off until twilight had dimmed everything to virtual obscurity. At that point, I would gather all the lamps from the lounge and bedrooms onto the kitchen counter and arrange them in a row. Having checked for any that needed re-filling, I removed the glass chimneys, carefully placing them behind their bases, and turned up the wicks. Then, striking one long match, I would light each lamp in turn, and try to do the whole row before the match burnt my finger tips. I never managed it somehow and always had to strike a second one to light the last few. I've often thought how curious it was that I kept upholding the challenge to myself, even after repeatedly having to nurse scorched digits. I loved the sharp, acrid smell of the flaring matches, and strangely, I even enjoyed the slightly cloying fumes of the paraffin we used. It was part of everything I thought of as home.

After replacing the chimneys, I made sure to adjust the wicks so that the flame made an almost perfect arc and the light spilled gently onto the pine worktop from the grouped collection of lamps. This done, I slowly and carefully carried them to their designated spots, invariably looking with pleasure on the soft golden glow that emanated from each shiny glass tube. It was such an immensely satisfying task.

I loved these lamps, even though they were hopelessly impractical and we couldn't really see properly to do anything other than read with heads and books dipped towards the circles of light. Bill and I fitted our lives to their luminary limitations and I took up knitting, which I barely needed to look at, while he polished tools or cleaned parts of his precious motorbike. I even read bedtime stories to the girls with a book in one hand and a lamp in the other. For our own entertainment, we had a radio, so we didn't mind the fact that everything away from the orbit of the light was in deep shadow, even ourselves. We could listen as we worked, completely contented.

In the winter, the wood fire burning in the wide hearth supplemented the lamp light and our Swiss-style room was bathed in a warm rosy glow reminiscent of the most romantic of film sets. At some point, although I don't quite remember when, we bought banjos, and started teaching ourselves to play, and then I had my guitar, for which I already had quite a repertoire. All of this was possible by lamp light as we needed no electricity to generate our own music.

As our stay on the farm stretched into years, we became so accustomed to our soft and limited lighting system that when we visited friends with electricity, their rooms always seemed to me to be unnecessarily bright. Like over-exposed photos, they felt harsh and unfriendly. I was always glad to go home; to gather my collection of cut-glass lamps together and go through the comforting ritual of testing my wick lighting skills once more with the flourish of a single burning match.

The scent of baked earth

Africa has its own scent. It is immediately and pungently noticeable the moment you step out of an aircraft onto its sun baked soil. Europe is green, moist and fresh, but Africa has a hypnotic, spicy, aroma that catches your breath. If a smell can have a colour, then the smell of Africa is terracotta – like the hue of its warm, dry, vibrantly red-brown earth.

On our mountain in Natal, the mists often came down to shroud us in a ghostly, silent world punctuated only by the dripping of leaves soaked in the saturated air. On these days, the earthy baked quality of the scent would be replaced by the sharper, keener tang of damp wattle needles and the drenched kikuyu grass. Other aromas would emerge too: the sweet but heavy stench of cow pats, normally masked or dried out by the heat; the fusty odour of wet dogs, sheep and cattle; the fresh scents released from the sandy surfaces of the road or the stone slabs of the veranda. They all seemed to compete for dominance in the air as if knowing that the return of the heat would find them subdued once more by Africa's typical all enveloping musk.

In the spring, the garden was filled with perfume from the climbing jasmine. Anyone who knows this fragrant, head spinning scent must agree it is one of nature's gifts. It is simply heavenly, and in Africa, it is infinitely more intense than in the softer climes of Europe. Winter brought the choking assault on the nose of burnt grass and scorched trees from the firebreaks or, if we were unlucky, the *veld* fires. Summer simultaneously washed, cooked, dried and hardened the land so that the spicy warmth that

156

became so familiar to me embedded itself deeply into the pores of the earth. If I close my eyes and focus, I can still conjure up its smell at will, and whenever I return to South Africa, it is with the first intake of breath that I feel I am home again.

The world in a radio

There were a number of radio stations we could receive on our mountain, and we listened in turn to all of them, including the SABC's main service and the Capitol Radio of Port St John's fame. My firm and absolute favourite, though, was Springbok Radio which provided me with a feast in daily entertainment.

We had a typical 'tranny': a battery operated transistor radio/cassette player which was small enough to cart around from room to room whatever I was doing. Most of the day, it lived on the kitchen counter and Springbok Radio served up my daily listening with a wonderful reliability that made almost every hour one of eager anticipation.

In the morning, there was the usual going-to-work sort of drive-time news and music show, but as soon as the rush hour could decently be expected to be over, the programmes of real substance started. Firstly, there was a half hour session with the case files of a psychiatrist whose name escapes me now and even extensive delving hasn't turned up. It was presented as something of a daily soap, but was compelling all the same. Then we had a variety of different programmes taking us through the day from self-help guidance talks to crazy comedy shows such as The Navy Lark and Men from the Ministry. In the afternoons, there was nearly always a radio drama, to which I listened avidly, sometimes stopping what I was doing in mid stir or brush stroke to concentrate on a moment of serious tension or excitement. Then the evenings brought the real feasts: Squad Cars, a police drama series; Inspector Carr Investigates, a detective series; Best Sellers, a dramatised serialisation of well-known novels by authors such as Dick Francis and Desmond Bagley. To add depth and education to our lives, there were also quiz programmes like The Three Wise Men. It was a treasure trove of entertainment and there wasn't a soul I knew who didn't love Springbok Radio.

Bill and I listened together in the evenings and I had it on all the time I was at home during the day. I was even known to cry off social events if it meant missing an episode of a favoured serial. I've never known a radio station quite like it. I was as hooked as any TV junkie, so much so that whenever I transport myself back to the farm in my mind's eye, it is curious that the first thing I see is our mountain home shrouded in mist with myself working at some kind of home industry in the kitchen. In these flashbacks, I am always accompanied by the friendly voices issuing from the studios of Springbok Radio. Somehow these pictures and this sound are synonymous with comfort and contentment, which in turn, are a pretty accurate reflection of how I felt about life on that far off Natalian mountain side.

Christmas

The festive season seemed all wrong to me at first. Upside down, inside out and totally reversed from what it should have been. Like the negative of a photo. The basis of the problem was of course because it is summer at Christmas in the southern hemisphere, and being a northerner, I was not used to Christmas carols and Santa in thirty-five degrees of heat. It is also the main annual holiday season, meaning that many firms and businesses shut down for the month of December. You may as well write off any attempts to get anything important done during the weeks leading up to the New Year.

It took some getting used to. Instead of snuggling round a fire indoors to open our presents, we were in shorts and tee-shirts round the *braai* in the garden. Christmas shopping was achieved at ludicrous levels of heat instead of fighting through crowds wrapped in scarves and woolly hats. Nevertheless, I did get used to it. I loved it eventually – the entire, crazy contradiction of it all.

The tantalising smells of wood smoke and charcoal grilled meat which has been decorated with holly and model snowmen; the enveloping, penetrating warmth of the sun on our skin, and then the incongruous strains of Christmas carols wafting on the air; the absurdity of shop windows filled with fake snow and Santa and his reindeer, while the window shoppers themselves are scantily clad in the briefest of everything. Christmas trees and candles by swimming pools and sunbeds. Midnight mass and festive street lights with floodlit cricket matches and beach games. None of it made any real sense to me. It was, and still is, all about a colonial culture clinging on to the traditions of its roots, but it was all embraced with so much enthusiasm that I came to enjoy it as much as anyone.

We too had our Christmas tree with lights. I bought aerosol snow, and made decorations from pine cones and silver spray paint. Looking back, I took more trouble over my 'winter' decorations in South Africa than I ever had in the real winters of England. It does me good, even now, to recall Christmas day on the beach at Port St Johns. Two small girls sun kissed and drowsy after an afternoon clambering over rocks and splashing naked in the sandy pools; a tired and mellow sun slipping down behind the horizon; a day that combined the seasonal traditions of goodwill and gift-giving of our former home with the benefits offered by the benevolent climate of our adoptive country. They were contradictions indeed, but when compounded they enhanced the pleasure of simply being. If the spirit of Christmas is about loving and giving, it was not difficult for me to achieve in such surroundings. As I said, I loved it.

The dragon's teeth

The last memory I have of Cottingham farm is of standing in the garden and watching the clouds spilling over the jagged points of the Drakensberg mountains way over to the west. I never tired of this view. It was constantly changing, shifting shape with the angles of the sun and the shadows cast by the clouds.

We could dispense with weather forecasts just by watching our section of the 'Dragon's teeth'. Most of our dramatic thunder-storms came from the Berg, and we could monitor their progress by the rate at which the great cumulus clouds rolled across the range. Then in the winter, there would be the excitement of seeing white caps on the points and slopes, adding a sharper definition to certain ribs and outcrops. If the white covering extended far enough down, we would even jump in the car and along with many other Natalians, head for the Sani Pass just to catch a close-up of that regional rarity: real snow.

160

In the mornings, the mountains always seemed to be much closer to us, an illusion no doubt caused by the direction of the light and the clarity of the morning skies. By late afternoon, they had receded into the distance, losing their detail to a deep purple haze and diminishing in size as if they had somehow sunk into the valleys around them.

The Berg provided the focal point and fullest extent of my view. I had this wonderful sensation of being able to stretch my eyes, but at the same time, relax them in the uncluttered expanse of the foothills that rose wave upon wave to meet the far off mountains.

Of all the precious images and memories of the farm I hold so dear, it is this that gives me the deepest and most lasting pleasure. On my first daylight visit to Cottingham, I looked out to the Berg and knew that I would never live anywhere as awe inspiringly beautiful as this ever again, and so far, to this day, that remains an unbroken truth.

It is perhaps fitting that the farm itself has gone now. Its fortunes were determined by various administrative manoeuvres, some of which could be regarded as mere expedients, but the outcome is that it is now submerged under a vast belt of land owned by a forestry company. Were it still there, I would hanker to return and that would inevitably be a mistake as the people I loved have also gone. However, in writing these chapters I have had the pleasure of re-living many of the episodes that made the life and those who filled it so precious. I have also had the benefit of hindsight, and realise how very fortunate I was to live there at that time.

The people who surrounded me then were all the products of what was a social and political *fait accompli*. Nevertheless, within our world, there was a deep affection and mutual respect, indeed a symbiosis, which is sadly lacking in most modern societies. In many ways, we were so isolated in our mountain kingdom that we were not only technologically cut off from the twentieth century, but we were blessedly also social castaways, meaning we could develop our relationships as we wished.

So it is, then, that I would like to dedicate these final pages to the memory of my favourite 'characters' on the farm: the Ellenses and Gwen of course, but even more importantly to Kheswa, Bongi, May and of course Jacob, the inimitable pot-watering gardener. A few of these precious souls have inevitably passed away, but I can only hope that those who remain are enjoying their own current version of African ways.

THE END

Valerie Poore

Read the first chapter of Valerie Poore's next book

WATERY WAYS

A memoir about her first year of living on a barge in the Netherlands

CHAPTER ONE

The Beginning Of It All

One of the first things you learn when living on a boat is that an awful lot of stuff is going to end up in the water. You also learn that it is a rather special way of life and, looking back, I wish I had come to it much earlier. Being now in what can only kindly be called my middle age, it seems rather late to have started a new love affair, but I can say with complete honesty that is what has happened. What's more, I have thrown caution to the winds with happy abandon and am about to embark on a whole new phase, living by myself on a historic barge in Rotterdam.

Initially, I came to the Netherlands to follow a husband who was in pursuit of one of his numerous career dreams. In South Africa, where I lived before Holland, we had owned our own homes. Not just apartments but real houses, on sizeable plots of land, with big gardens. Shock and disbelief set in when we realised the price of a modest house here could be compared to that of a millionaire's mansion in Johannesburg. We were not going to manage even so much as a lock-up garage on our limited means.

Ever creative, my then-husband started sowing other seeds. "Look at these canals," he said. "Wouldn't it be wonderful to live on a house boat?" he suggested tentatively. Knowing my aversion to all things cold and wet, he was being very brave to even hint at such a possibility. Nevertheless, the seeds found a fertile corner in my mind and I started watching the Dutch *binnenvaartschepen* (inland waterway barges) with some curiosity. As they ploughed their way up and down the rivers and canals I realised I liked what I saw. I became intrigued. Eventually, I became hooked on the idea.

What finally clinched it was the cost of buying a *woonschip* or houseboat. At first we looked at the more conventional *woonarken* which line many of the canals in most of the big cities. These are, in effect, floating houses. Some of them are built up on the hulls of old barges, but many of them are constructed on concrete bases and remain fixed to their moorings. I have to say that they are very appealing and often come with small gardens, but the price is usually as high as that of a standard house or apartment.

However, we had noticed that in some of the cities there are harbours designated for historic barges, which are also used for living aboard. The appeal of these old cargo-carrying boats is that they can still be used for travel, and the idea of going on holiday and taking my house with me was even more attractive. On investigation, it appeared that we could buy an old flat-bottomed barge for a fraction of the price of a normal house, so, given our love of all things antique and historic, this seemed like a good option. With kids grown and gone and only the dogs and cats to worry about, living space was no longer a major issue. Besides, on a barge you have the whole of the deck to expand onto as well, not to mention being a secure playground for our furry friends.

After several months search, we finally found what we wanted at a very reasonable price. The bad news was that to find a permanent mooring for it, we would have to undertake some major restoration work to make it acceptable in one of the historic harbours that we were so keen to live in. The barge we chose had a beautiful hull, but it had been modernised in the seventies and improved beyond repair. It had a kind of caravan structure built over the hold and, even worse, it had the ugliest wheelhouse I have ever seen. Historic harbour or not, this simply had to go.

To cut a long story short, finance for the restoration project was finally granted after much pleading and grovelling with several banks. Interestingly enough, it is not unusual to have a mortgage for a houseboat in the Netherlands, but the conditions are rather more stringent than they are for a house, and we were newcomers, both working as freelance business English teachers and with no track record – a risk in other words. Following the approval of our loan, and after re-naming it the *Kaapse Draai* (from a South African expression meaning a life changing U Turn), the barge was accepted into the Oude Haven in Rotterdam to undertake the project. All this was achieved with the help and support of some wonderful people we met in the harbour. Their kindness, humour and oddball approach to life cemented our belief that this was indeed, and at last, The Life.

At the end of February 2000, we were in. Then the problems began. Relations between my husband and I deteriorated from stable to rocky, and then into total collapse, precipitated mainly by the stress of the undertaking we had embarked on. I retreated from the fray and found myself grateful to be back in South Africa for a six-month spell of work. Its original intention was to help finance the restoration of the barge, but the extended break proved to be too much for an already floundering situation. My husband and I agreed to part.

The problem was, I was still in love with The Life. Depressed didn't even begin to describe how I felt about not living on a boat when I returned to the Netherlands. I even considered not going back at all but, with all my worldly possessions still there, I had little real choice. Then a heaven sent opportunity dropped into my email inbox a few weeks before I was due to fly back.

Before leaving for South Africa, I had spent three months helping one of the harbour dwellers to restore his wheelhouse. It was a labour of love for me as I have a passion for old wood, and the teak timberwork on these old barges was usually magnificent. In the process of this project, Philip, the owner, became a good friend, and I learnt that he owned three or four barges, all with berths in the neighbouring harbours.

Now word gets around fast in such a small community. It's a bit like the African bush telegraph. People seem to know what's going on like smells on the breeze, so news of my new status had obviously spread, even while I was thousands of kilometres away. To my delight, the email I received was from Philip, and he was offering me The Lifeline – did I want to stay on one of his barges if, and when, I came back?

What a question! I decided to give it a try for six months, thinking this should be long enough to see if I could make it alone in the Netherlands.

So it was that, with renewed determination and more than a little eager anticipation, I boarded the plane in

Johannesburg last night – at nine-thirty on the twenty-seventh of December 2000, to be precise.

The flight is long, but I am used to it after having made this trip several times before, and I have had plenty of time to reflect on what has led me to this point. Indeed, I am very much aware as I sit in my aisle seat on the great Boeing 747 that this is the first stage of the journey to begin my new life and education in watery ways.

In all possible ways, I am excited about the challenge, but there is a part of me that is nervous and fearful of the decision I have made. Still, it is far too late to turn back now

WATERY WAYS is available on Amazon
in both paperback and e-book formats.

ACKNOWLEDGEMENTS

I would like to thank all the faithful readers who followed the writing of these recollections on my Weblog, and gave me such encouraging feedback.

Of special note are: Anne Marie Klein, Gypsy Noir, Mary Beth, Maria from Finland, Renate Heins, 'Always the Wit' Guy, and the silent Alex. My daughters Jojo and Mo, who feature strongly in the pages that follow, have also been a great encouragement.

Lastly, I owe love and thanks to Koos, my partner, who has been my fearless editor throughout; fearless because he dared to give me criticism – but always of the constructive variety, of course

ABOUT THE AUTHOR

Valerie Poore was born in London, England, and grew up in both north London and the west of Dorset. After completing her degree in English, History and French at Bournemouth, she took a further course in the conservation and restoration of museum artefacts at Lincoln College of Art.

She then spent two years doing furniture restoration before going to South Africa in 1981 with her husband and small children.

Valerie left South Africa permanently in 2001 and has settled in the Netherlands, where she lives on a barge in

Rotterdam. She teaches academic and business English on a freelance basis and writes in her spare time.

She has completed nine books in total: the 'Ways' memoir series - African Ways is the first, followed by African Ways Again and Highveld Ways; then comes Watery Ways and Harbour Ways and Walloon Ways. There is also a travelogue titled Faring to France on a Shoe, as well as two novels: The Skipper's Child and How to Breed Sheep, Geese and English Eccentrics.

There is a further memoir in progress, which will be published this year (2020).

All Valerie's books are available as e-books and paperbacks.

Valerie Poore

Printed in Great Britain
by Amazon